MODELS-BASED TEACHING:

MODELS-BASED TEACHING:
AS EXCELLENT INNOVATIONS IN TEACHING

Dr. Sasmita Mohanty

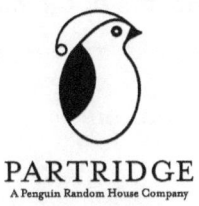

PARTRIDGE
A Penguin Random House Company

To order additional copies of this book, contact
Partridge India
000 800 10062 62
orders.india@partridgepublishing.com

www.partridgepublishing.com/india

Contents

Preface

The need and requirement of the children go on changing from time to time, environment to environment and from stage to stage. To keep pace with these changes a teacher must requires new knowledge, experience, skill and attitude to cater to the demands of the day and the present generation of pupils. In this respect a lot of research has been going on into theories of learning and application of these theories to the development of teaching strategies and models.

This book is an attempt to highlight the effectiveness of Models of Teaching in the development of Concept and Achievement of Primary school students. The author is thankful to the publication for publishing this book.

Dr. Sasmita Mohanty

1.0.0 INTRODUCTION

The foundation of any good system of education rests upon the quality of its elementary schools. In the days to come perhaps the schools may assume with some regard as a more scientific pasture and develop cluster curriculums that desire from more concentrated and pervasive intents. Thus, a parent might choose for his child a school that clustered its programme around a central purpose - such as academic achievement, life adjustment or personality development and he could make his choice from these more clearly defined areas of emphasis. The qualitative school brings into play a selective and powerful array of ideas. It has both depth and richness. Innovation or experimentation is one of the mark of a healthy school organism, which gives emphasis to the science subject. The chief element of quality in science lies in its capacity to develop scientific thinking in children. This forms an important part of the science programme in most schools, but lacks the degree of emphasis which it requires in order to be effective. It tends to become interwoven with other purposes and loses some of its strength in the process. The stating of multiple purposes for primary science, however, tends to obscure the unique and central role to be played by this aspect of the curriculum, thereby weakening its contribution. Beside this problem, the chief bit of nonsense which has wide currency among primary students is that science is terribly complicated and difficult subject. It is the lack of adequate preparation in science, rather than its inherent difficulty, which seems to create the problem of low achievement of the primary students in science subject.

The above discussion states that, in order to achieve the goals and expectations of the science education, only updating, revising, reorganising or adopting science curricula are not sufficient to reduce the present state of fragmentation and narrowness rather there is the requirement of more research studies on how and how much knowledge in science should be given to a child at primary stage. Therefore, the investigator took up an experimental research study to find out the effects of two models of teaching namely Concept Attainment Model and Advance Organiser Model in the development of concept and achievement in science of primary school students.

1.1.0 MODELS OF TEACHING

In the present modern scientific and technological world, importance is being given in the inclusion of various need based, psychological, relevant, dynamic and valid subjects in the curriculum for the growth and development of learners. More emphasis is given by the curriculum constructors on teaching than the learning. Various new theories, approaches, methods, models of teaching have been developed to make the learning effective, dynamic, significant, scientific and comprehensive.

A model of teaching consists of guidelines for designing educational activities and environments. It specifies ways of teaching and learning that are intended to achieve certain kinds of goals. According to Joyce and Weil, a teaching model is a pattern or plan which can be used to shape curriculum or course, to design instructional materials and to guide a teacher's actions. Thus, model of teaching like plans, patterns or blueprints present steps necessary to bring about a desired outcome.

Teaching model is a tentative theory of teaching. The best way to proceed in formulating a theory of teaching is to begin with what is known about learning in the classroom by adopting a model derived from a theory of learning. Hence, the models of teaching are just instructional designs. They describe the process of specifying and producing particular environment situation which cause the student to interact in such a way that specific change occurs in his behaviour and also we can realise how well they achieve the specific objectives towards which they can be directed and how well they increase the ability to learn, which is their fundamental purpose. Hence, the models of teaching are helpful in formulating and developing theory of teaching. Apart from the above uses it creates the necessary environment which facilitates the teaching process.

1.1.1 CHARACTERISTICS OF A GOOD MODEL

The following are the characteristics of a teaching model:

1. Some Assumptions: Each teaching model has certain basic elements which are kept in mind while models are developed. They are:

- (a) Creation of appropriate environment.
- (b) Occurrence of an interaction between a teacher and the pupils.
- (c) Using proper teaching strategies for making the teaching easy, clear and understandable.

2. Presenting Appropriate Experiences:
The second characteristic of a teaching model is, it provides proper experiences to both teacher and the pupil.

3. Answer to Fundamental Questions:
The model of teaching provides answer to all the fundamental questions. For example (a) How does a teacher behave? (b) Why he does like this? and (c) What would be the effects of his such behaviour on the pupils? In other words, it answers all the fundamental questions pertaining to the behaviour of teachers and pupils are received.

4. Based on Individual Differences:
It is constructed on the basis of individual differences and according to various assumptions, which gives importance to the clarification of concepts.

5. Use of Student's Interest:
The fifth characteristic of a teaching model is to looks after the interest of the pupils.

6. Influenced by Philosophy:
The models of teaching are influenced by the philosophy of life. For example: teacher constructs a teaching model to change the behaviour of the pupils.

7. Qualitative Development of Teacher's Personality:
The main feature of teaching models is that they bring about the qualitative development of the teacher's personality.

1.1.2 FUNCTIONS OF A TEACHING MODEL

The following are the functions of a teaching model:

1. It helps a teacher to develop his capacity to teach more children and creates conducive environment for them.
2. It helps curriculum makers to plan learning centre and curriculum which provides a variety of educational experiences to children.
3. It helps to create more interesting and effective instructional materials and learning sources.
4. It stimulates the development of new educational forms.
5. It helps to formulate a theory of teaching.

1.1.3   ELEMENTS OF A MODEL

A teaching model has six fundamental elements, they are:

(i) Focus: Focus refers to the goals or objectives of teaching or a frame of references, which is the central aspect of a teaching model. Objectives of teaching and aspects of the environment generally constitute the focus of the model.

(ii) Syntax: A syntax refers to the description of the model in action or structure of activities and also includes the sequence of steps involved in the organisation of the complete programme of teaching. Hence, it indicates the shape of the activities which specify educational environment relating to each model.

(iii) Principles of reactions: This element is concerned with the way a teacher should regard and respond to the activities of the students, it means it refers to flexibility or rigidity of teaching. These responses should be appropriate and selective.

(iv) Social System: It is related to the description of the following: (a) Interactive roles and relationship between the teacher and the students. (b) The kinds of norms that are observed and students behaviour which is rewarded.

(v) Support System: The support system related to the additional requirements other than the usual human skills or capacities of the teacher and facilities usually available in the ordinary classroom. These additional requirements refer to special skills and special knowledge of the teacher to implement the strategy of teaching.

(vi) Application Context: There are availability of several types of teaching models. Each model attempts to describe the feasibility of its use in varying contexts-goal achievement-cognitive, affective and psychomotor domains.

1.2.0 FAMILIES OF MODELS

Bruce Joyce and Marsha Weil (1985) organised these models into the following four families on the basis of their chief emphasis - the way they approach educational goals and means. They are given in below:

1. Behaviour Modification Models
2. Information Processing Models
3. Personal Models
4. Social Interaction Models

1.2.1 BEHAVIOUR MODIFICATION MODELS

Behaviour Modification Models of learning and instruction have their origins in the classical conditioning experiments of Pavlov (1927), the work of Thorndike on reward learning (1898, 1911, 1913) and the studies of Watson and his associates, who applied Pavlov's principles of the psychological disorders of human beings. Skinner is the chief exponent of this model. He argues that human behaviour can be understood in terms of the principles of operant conditioning and whole stresses roles of classical conditioning in changing human behaviour.

The Behaviour Modification Models give stress in changing the external behaviour of the learners and describe them in terms of visible behaviour rather than underlying behaviour. These models are generally based on the principles of stimulus control and reinforcement and it can be employed on both individual and on a group.

1.2.2 INFORMATION PROCESSING MODELS

The Information Processing Models focus in the development of the capacity in the students through the processing of information and the teaching objectives. The Information Processing Models refer to the way people handle stimuli from the environment, organise data, sense problems, generate concepts and solve problems and use verbal and nonverbal symbols. Models of this type are concerned with the intellectual growth rather than the emotional or social environment.

1.2.3 PERSONAL DEVELOPMENT MODELS

Personal Development Model assists the individual in self development. Frequently, they also focus on the emotional life of an individual. Thus, the Personal Development Model emphasises the processes by which individuals establish productive relationship with their environment and design their unique individuality. Efforts have been made to develop individuals self-hood culminating into self actualisation.

1.2.4 SOCIAL INTERACTION MODELS

Social Interaction Models stress the relationship of the individual to other person to other society. The main aim of these models are to develop social efficiency among the pupils and also give priority to social relations and creation of an ideal society.

1.3.0 CONCEPT ATTAINMENT MODEL

In 1956, the Concept Attainment Model of teaching was developed by Jerome S. Bruner, Jacqueline Goorow and Geroge Austin. This model has been developed from the "Study of Thinking". It is based on the assertion that environment is full of tremendously diverse things and it would have been impossible to adjust in it if human beings had not been endowed with the capacity to discriminate and to categorise things in group benefits human beings in three ways. First, it reduces the complexity of the environment. Secondly, it gives the means by which we can identify the objects in the world and thirdly, it reduces the necessity of constant learning. In other words, having learned concepts, one is able to identify the others examples of the concept without further learning. The internal conditions of concept learning are the ability to discriminate between objects and the ability to notice commonalties in them. Contiguity, repetition and feedback are some internal conditions.

1.3.1 VIEW ON CONCEPT

Generally, a concept may be free to be class or category of all the members of which share particular combination of attributes or critical properties not shared by another class. Hence, a concept is consists of an individual to discriminate a particular thing or class of things and also relate it to other things or classes of things. According to Bruner (1956) a concept is a class or group response of an act of categorisation, involves rendering, discriminate different things equivalent to the group of the objects and events and people around us into classes to respond to them in terms of their class membership rather than their uniqueness.

1.3.2 ELEMENTS OF A CONCEPT

According to Bruner every concept has five elements that mean these elements help us to understand a concept. The elements are discussed below:

(i) Name: Name is a term given to a category. For example: book, bird, cat, circle etc. are all names given to a range of objects or experiences, which enables the children to understand a concept easily and also they can express their experiences perfectly.

(ii) Examples: Examples are instances of the concept. Examples can be positive or negative. In teaching a concept, it is important to present examples with
non-examples. So that the students can identify examples from non-examples.

(iii) Attribute: An attribute is a characteristic of an object which differentiates it from the others. Colour, texture, form, size, number of parts, position and sound are examples of attributes. Every concept has two types of attributes,

(a) Essential attributes: Essential attributes are the common features or characteristics of a concept. These attributes should be present in all examples of the concept.

(b) Non-essential attributes: Some of the slight differences among examples of the category reflect the non-essential attributes.

(iv) Attribute Value: Each attribute has an attribute value or several values. For example, colour may be as attribute and red, yellow, green etc. are the attribute values. Different things are put into categories on the basis of attribute values.

(v) Definition: The last element of the concept is the definition or rule. A definition or rule is a statement specialising the attributes of a concept. A correct rule helps in the successful utilisation of the other elements of a concept.

1.3.3   STRATEGIES OF CONCEPT ATTAINMENT MODEL

Burner's valuable insights deserves our consideration because his view of the child as an information processor, thinker and creator emphasis both rationality and dignity. So, according to him, if teachers respect a child's thinking process and translate material into meaningful units, they should join mental growth, modes of representation and learning processes together to introduce great ideas to children at different times and with increasing abstractness. Basically three types of strategies are used for teaching through Concept Attainment Model namely

- The Reception Oriented Model
- The Selection Oriented Model

In the present study the researcher has chosen the Reception Oriented Model of concept attainment. Thus, the description of only Reception Oriented Model is given below:

1.3.4   DESCRIPTION OF RECEPTION ORIENTED MODEL OF CONCEPT ATTAINMENT

(i) Syntax of the Reception Oriented Model of concept attainment

Phase - I: Presentation of data and identification of concept

The teacher presents labelled 'Yes' and 'No' examples arranged from simple to more difficult. Students compare the attributes of examples and non-examples in order to identify the common attributes of 'Yes' examples. Then, they state the definition or rule according to the essential attributes. Students also formulate the hypothesis of a concept.

Phase - II: Testing attainment of the concept

The students are presented unlabeled examples and are asked to identify those examples that are the correct examples of the concept. The students are also required to generate their own examples and thereby confirm or reject their hypothesis about the concept.

Phase - III: Analysis of thinking strategy

The students discuss and describe thoughts and hypothesis among themselves and analyse the problems through which they attain the concept and their thinking processes were analysed and discussed.

(ii) Social system:

In the Concept Attainment Model of teaching, the teacher is the controller of the learning because the teacher chooses the concept, selects and organise the material into positive and negative examples and sequences the examples. In most cases teachers will have to prepare examples, extracting ideas and materials from texts and other sources, but designing them in such a way that the attributes are clear and that there are both negative and positive examples of the concept. During this phase the teacher performs three major functions. Those are, to record, prompt and present additional data as needed. This stage is very helpful for the learner's intellectual development.

(iii) Principles of reaction:

During the teaching-learning process the teacher supports the hypothesis formulated by the students by emphasising that they should be hypothetical in nature and also create a dialogue in which the major content is to balance one person's hypothesis against another. There is a focus of specific feature of each example.

In the later phases of the model, the teacher must turn the student's attention towards analysis of their concepts and their thinking strategies with proper assistance.

(iv) Support system:

Support system consists of material that has been designed so that concepts are embedded in the material, with positive and negative examples that can be pointed out to the students. In this model, students do not invent new concepts, but attain the one that have previously been selected by the teacher. Hence, the data sources need to be known before hand and the aspects of concept attainment activity made visible.

(v) Application of the model:

This phase can be used with students from upper primary classes onwards. Further, the Reception Model is very appropriate for young children whereas the selection and unorganised strategies are more useful in secondary grades. The model is also an excellent tool for evaluation. The phase two of the model, tests the attainment of the concepts by asking for additional examples and labelling the given examples.

1.4.0   ADVANCE ORGANISER MODEL

Teaching is not everybody's tea cup to sip. It is an art and skill to be learnt. It requires the knowledge of subject content, method, techniques and teaching aids to be used for making teaching interesting and effective and also to bring desirable changes in the behaviour of the learner. For that purpose only the teacher has to employ new teaching strategies in the classrooms. Advance Organiser Model, which occupied a vital place in the teaching-learning process. Because the most important aim of Advance Organiser Model is to improve the instructional effectiveness through an interactive atmosphere.

Advance Organiser Model was developed and systematically studied by David Ausubel in 1960. This theory of learning is also known as the 'Theory of Meaningful Learning'. Ausubel is one of the few educational psychologists to address learning, teaching and curriculum simultaneously. His theory of meaningful verbal learning deals with three concerns (1) how knowledge (curriculum/content) is organised, (2) how the mind works to process new information (learning) and (3) how teachers can apply these ideas about curriculum and learning when they present new materials to students (instruction). Hence, Ausubel's primary concern is to help teachers to organise and convey large amounts of information as meaningfully and effectively as possible. Advance Organiser Model was based on Ausubel's 'Theory of Meaningful Verbal Learning'.

1.4.1   CONCEPT OF ADVANCE ORGANISER

An Advance Organiser is a cognitive instructional strategy used to promote the learning and retention of new information. According to Ausubel, these organisers are introduced in advance of learning itself and are also presented at a higher level of abstraction, generality and inclusiveness. Their purpose is to explain, integrate and interrelate the materials in the learning tasks with previously learned materials. The most effective organisers are those that use concepts, terms and propositions that are already familiar to the learners, as well as appropriate illustrations and analogies.

Hence, advance organisers present a higher level of abstraction. They are not just simple overviews, illustrating examples etc. But they share with such techniques the idea, that they must be integrated with other teaching-learning activities. Therefore, organisers act as a bridge between new learning material and existing related ideas.

1.4.2 CHARACTERISTICS OF ADVANCE ORGANISER MODEL

The simple characteristics behind Advance Organiser Model are that:

(1) Most general ideas should be presented first in an organised way and then progressively differentiated.
(2) Following instructional materials should integrate new concepts with previously presented information and with an overall organisation.
(3) Provide a means of generating logical relationship among elements.
(4) Influence the learner's encoding process.
(5) Short set of verbal or visual informations.

1.4.3 TYPES OF ADVANCE ORGANISER MODEL

There are two types of Advance Organisers:

(i) Expository Organisers
(ii) Comparative Organisers

(i) Expository Organisers

Expository Organisers provide a basic concept at the highest level of abstraction and perhaps some lesser concepts. These represent the intellectual scaffold on which students will 'hang' the new information as they encounter it. Expository Organisers are especially helpful because they provide ideational scaffolding for familiar material.

(ii) Comparative Organisers

Comparative Organisers on the other hand, are used most with relatively familiar material. They are designed to integrate new concepts with basically similar concepts existing in the cognitive structure. They are also designed to discriminate between the old and new concepts in order to prevent confusion caused by their similarity.

1.4.4   STRATEGIES OF ADVANCE ORGANISER MODEL

Advance Organiser Model is highly useful in the process of transferring knowledge. Because of the deductive reasoning, students are able to use the rule than the example for learning to occur. Mayer writes in his text, "... the affect of advance organisers should be must visible for tests that involve creative problem solving or transfer to new situations, because the Advance Organiser Model allows the learner to organise the material into a familiar structure". (Mayer, 2003).

In this model the teacher provides an advance organiser and he provides a set of hang pins termed as 'Intellectual scaffolding', a structure on which the learner can hang the ideas and facts which they would be presented during the lessons teacher uses the advance organiser that they already knew. Expository Model has been most frequently used. The books and reading materials also follow predominantly in expository presentation of the learning task. The purpose of this model is to equip the teacher to convey information meaningfully as it is one of the goal of the school. The lecture is to be organised in a way.

1.4.5   DESCRIPTION OF ADVANCE ORGANISER MODEL

(i) Syntax of the Advance Organiser Model

Phase - I: Presentation of advance organiser

The teacher clarify aims of the lessons, present organiser: Identify defining attributes, give examples, provide multi-context, repeat, prompt awareness of learner's relevant knowledge and experience in learners background.

Phase - II: Presentation of the learning task

The teacher presents material to students, maintain attention, make organisation explicit, make logical order of learning material explicit.

Phase - III: Strengthening cognitive organisation

The teacher uses principles of integrative reconciliation, prompt active reception learning, elicit critical approach to subject matter and clarify.

Syntax:

Phase one:

During this phase, first of all the objectives are explained and clarified and after which the advance organiser is presented to the students. Whether the organiser is expository or comparative, the essential features of the concept or proposition must be pointed out. The presentation of an organiser must be perceived, clearly understood and continually related to the material it is organising. Finally, it is important to prompt awareness of the learner's prior knowledge and experiences that might be relevant to this learning task and organiser.

Phase two:

In phase two, the learning materials are presented in the form of lecturers, discussions, films, experiments or reading. During the presentation, the organisation of the learning material needs to be made explicit to the students. So that, they have an overall sense of direction and can see the logical order of the material and how the organisation relates to the advance organiser. Attempts are made to maintain motivation and interests.

Phase three:
At this stage, the cognitive material is strengthened. The purpose of this stage is to anchor new material with old. That is, 'integrative' reconciliation is brought about. This is brought about by asking the students to prepare the summary of major attributes of new materials, repeat definitions and ask students to differentiate the closely related subjects.

(ii) Social System:
In this model, the teacher retains control of the intellectual structure as it is necessary continually to relate the learning material to the organisers and to help students differentiate new material from previously learned material.

(iii) Principles of reaction:
The teacher is seen as presenter of the learning material. The teacher's reaction will be guided by the purpose of clarifying the meaning of the new learning material, differentiating it from and reconciling it with existing knowledge, making it personally relevant to the student and helping to promote a critical approach to knowledge.

(iv) Support system:
Well organised material is the critical support requirement of this model. The effectiveness of the advance organiser depends on an integrate and appropriate relationship between the conceptual organiser and the context. This model provides guidelines for building instructional materials.

(v) Application of the model:

The Advance Organiser Model is especially useful to structure extended curriculum sequences or systematically in the key ideas of a field. It increases the learner's grasp of factual information linked to and explained by the key ideas.

1.5.0 RATIONALE OF THE STUDY

The rapid advancement of science and technology and increasing need for scientists and technologists have made it all the more important to provide for science based education in the schools. Now science has been recognised as a compulsory right from the elementary stage and now one of the core subjects at Higher Secondary Stage, which helps the pupil to gain a basic quantum of scientific knowledge as a part of his general education. In this context, Kothari Commission (1964 - 66) stated that, "we lay great emphasis on making science an important element in the school curriculum. We, therefore, recommend that science should be taught on a compulsory basis to all pupils as a part of general education during the first ten years of schooling. In addition, there should be provision of special courses in these subjects at the secondary stage for students of more than average ability".

The subject science is so valuable and psychologically based, which is so closely connected with our daily life. As science education develops well defined abilities and values such as the spirit of enquiry, creativity, objectivity, the courage to question and an aesthetic sensibility in the child, it occupies an important place in our curriculum. At the primary stage, science gives emphasis on the acquisition of knowledge and the ability to think logically, to draw conclusions and to make decisions at a higher level. But, it has been realised that our primary school children are unable to do expected result in science. Several factors may be responsible for low achievement of students in science. But one of the important factor is the application of ineffective teaching strategies by the teacher. In this regard, Kothari Commission Report (1964 - 66) states, "if science is poorly taught and badly learn, it is little more than burdening the mind with dead information and it could degenerate even into a new superstitions". Hence, in order to improve the achievement level of the primary students in science, there is the requirement of adoption of new, effective and efficient teaching strategies by the science teachers.

For the present investigation the investigator has selected two teaching strategies namely Concept Attainment Model and Advance Organiser Model from the area of models of teaching for the development of concepts and achievement in science of primary school students.

1.6.0 STATEMENT OF THE PROBLEM

For the present study the problem is stated as follows:

"A study of effectiveness of Concept Attainment Model and Advance Organiser Model in the development of concept and achievement in science of primary school students".

1.7.0 OPERATIONAL DEFINITIONS

1.7.1 DEVELOPMENT OF CONCEPT IN SCIENCE

A concept is defined as the form categorising a number of observation. According to Bruner, a concept is a class or grouping response, an act of categorisation, involves rendering different things equivalent. Concepts involve the ability of persons to distinguish between objects, so that they are classified as belonging or not belonging to a particular group of objects. According to Bruner any concept possess five elements like name, example (+ve, -ve), attributes or characteristics, attribute value and rule or definition. Hence, learning of concept implies acquiring knowledge and understanding of the above five elements of the concept.

1.7.2 ACHIEVEMENT IN SCIENCE

In the school situations, an Achievement Test is used as a tool for measuring the nature and extent of student learning in a particular subject or group of subjects. However a particular student has been able to learn and acquire or has been benefited from the learning experiences given to him ascertained with the help of Achievement Test. Therefore, Achievement Test is essentially post-oriented. It gives evidences of what has been learned or acquired by an individual by testing his present ability. In other words, we can define, an Achievement Test as an essential tool or device of measurement that helps in ascertaining quantity and quality of learning attained in a subject of study or group of subjects after a period of instruction by measuring the present ability of the individual concerned.

In the present investigation, the investigator has followed two instructional strategies namely Concept Attainment Model and Advance Organiser Model to test achievement in science of class - IV students. For this purpose, some topics from unit II to IX of class - IV science text book were identified for instructing the students of class - IV through Concept Attainment Model and Advance Organiser Model.

Before treatments applied in the experimental groups, Achievement Test in science consisting of 40 marks was administered on the students of experimental and control groups. After the presentation of 30 lessons in the experimental and control groups post-tests were administered to find out the effectiveness of both the treatments on the achievement of the students in science. So, the achievement of students in science refers to the increase of the test scores from pre-test to post-test after treatment. On the other words, the achievement of the students means measuring the differences between the pre-test and post-test scores after the treatment in the Achievement Test.

1.8.0 OBJECTIVES OF THE STUDY

The following objectives have been undertaken:

1. To study the effectiveness of Concept Attainment Model in the concept development of primary students in science.
2. To study the effectiveness of Concept Attainment Model in the achievement of primary students in science.
3. To study the effectiveness of Advance Organiser Model in the concept development of primary students in science.
4. To study the effectiveness of Advance Organiser Model in the achievement of primary students in science.
5. To study the comparative effectiveness of Concept Attainment Model and Advance Organiser Model in the concept development of primary students in science.
6. To study the comparative effectiveness of Concept Attainment Model and Advance Organiser Model in the achievement of primary students in science.
7. To study the difference in the concept development between boys and girls taught through Concept Attainment Model in science.
8. To study the difference in the achievement between boys and girls taught through Concept Attainment Model in science.
9. To study the difference in the concept development between boys and girls taught through Advance Organiser Model in science.
10. To study the difference in the achievement between the boys and girls taught through Advance Organiser Model in science.
11. To study the relationship between intelligence and concept development.
12. To study the relationship between intelligence and achievement.
13. To study the relationship between concept development and achievement.

1.9.0   HYPOTHESIS OF THE STUDY

The following hypotheses have been undertaken:

1. There is no significant difference in the Mean Concept Development Test Gain Scores of Experimental Group - I (Ex1) and Control Group - I (C1).
2. There is no significant difference in the Mean Achievement Test Gain Scores of Experimental Group - I (Ex1) and Control Group - I (C1).
3. There is no significant difference in the Mean Concept Development Test Gain Scores of Experimental Group - II (Ex2) and Control Group - II (C2).
4. There is no significant difference in the Mean Achievement Test Gain Scores of Experimental Group - II (Ex2) and Control Group - II (C2).
5. There is no significant difference in the Mean Concept Development Test Gain Scores between Experimental Group - I (Ex1) and Experimental Group - II (Ex2).
6. There is no significant difference in the Mean Achievement Test Gain Scores of Experimental Group - I (Ex1) and Experimental Group - II (Ex2).
7. There is no significant difference in the Mean Concept Development Test Gain Scores between boys and girls taught through Concept Attainment Model.
8. There is no significant difference in the Mean Achievement Test Gain Scores between boys and girls taught through Concept Attainment Model.
9. There is no significant difference in the Mean Concept Development Test Gain Scores between boys and girls taught through Advance Organiser Model.
10. There is no significant difference in the Mean Achievement Test Gain Scores of boys and girls taught through Advance Organiser Model.
11. There is no significant correlation between Intelligence and Concept Development Test Scores.

12. There is no significant correlation between Intelligence and Achievement Test Scores.
13. There is no significant correlation between Concept Development Test and Achievement Test Scores.

1.10.0 DELIMITATIONS OF THE STUDY

The following delimitations were made for the present study:

1. The present study is restricted to a comparative study of two models of teaching, namely, Concept Attainment Model and Advance Organiser Model.
2. The study is confined to the primary students studying science as a compulsory subject.
3. Only the class - IV Students of primary school has been selected as the sample for the purpose of experimentation.
4. Only the class - IV students of Baripada Municipality in the District of Mayurbhanj, is taken as sample of the study.
5. Schools providing Co-education have been undertaken for the investigation.
6. The population of the study is consist of four groups. Therefore, the sample of the study was restricted to 107 students only.
7. Both the standardised and Teacher-made test have been used in the present study.

2.0.0 INTRODUCTION

The purpose of the review of literature is to buildup in the context and background of the research as well as to provide a basis for formation of the hypothesis. Above all, the reviews gave very clear insight into the study area, enabling the researcher to define the objectives, the scope, measurement and methodology. By reviewing the literature the researcher not only delimits and defines her problem but also she can avoid duplicating well established findings. As model of teaching is a new area introduced in India, it needs more experiment to know the effectiveness of its different models at various levels of teaching. The researcher collected a number of research studies under the area of Concept Attainment Model and Advance Organiser Model of teaching.

2.1.0 RESEARCH STUDIES IN INDIA OF CONCEPT ATTAINMENT MODEL

Antimadas (1986) developed the model competency of pre-service teacher trainees by adopting Concept Attainment Model with three different training strategies. The sample consisted of 55 B.Ed. students of the Education Department of Devi Ahilya Viswavidyalya, Indore, 16 P.F. Cattell, Teaching Analysis Guide (TAG) by Bruice Joyce, Factorial Analysis of Variance with unequal cell size and one-way ANOVA were utilised. He found that the three different training strategies were equally effective in terms of model competency of teacher-trainees at the end of the training and coaching stage.

Dr. Sasmita Mohanty

Bihari (1986) studied the effectiveness of three training strategies in learning Concept Attainment Model in terms of teaching competency of student-teachers, in terms of understanding of the mode, in terms of coaching through the model, in terms of reaction towards the model and in terms of willingness to implement the model. The sample consisted of 55 students-teachers studying in B.Ed. 'B' section of the Department of Education, D.A.V., Indore. He found that the three training strategies, namely, peer feedback and practice in quardo, peer feedback, and practice in pairs and demonstration followed by practice in quardo were equally effective for developing teaching competence.

Sharma (1986) studied the effectiveness of Concept Attainment Model in terms of achievement of students on attainment test based on the concepts taught in chemistry and the effectiveness of Concept Attainment Model in term of reactions of students towards the new method of teaching. Sample consisted of 67 students of Class IX from Kamla Nehru Girls' Higher Secondary School, Indore. He found that the mean performance of the experimental and control groups on achievement test is not significantly different from each other.

Pani (1988) compared the Concept Attainment Scores (CAS) of groups through Reception and Selection Strategies of concept attainment; and studied the effect of personality factors. The sample consisted of 30 students of Class VIII in Gramin Jiwan Jayoti School at Rao. He found that the Reception Strategy and Selection Strategy were equally effective in terms of attainment of science concept.

Pillai, A. S. (1989) studied the various measures of concept learning. Objectives were to study the structure, attributes and their interdependence, and the hierarchy of the concept-learning process. In methodology, it is a study based on the review of issues analysing the concepts process, concept structures, concept memory and explores application of Band theory of solids/energy for building Band Theory model of memory. Major findings were (i) concept learning may vary from person to person, (ii) every concept has a structure, (iii) concept understanding will greatly depend upon one's information about it, (iv) concept understanding keeps on changing, as more and more information is made available, (v) concept mastery is decided by concept evolving, concept understanding, concept application and concept memory, (vi) the Band Theory model of memory explains how certain information is easily retrieved while others are not, (vii) the model has developed with the help of scientific analogy taking fully into consideration all the existing theories, and (viii) through the model has accepted many things from the network models and psycho-analytic models, it suggests that no information is at the same level and it is organised in perfect hierarchical order. [KCN 1449].

Bawa, M.S. (1991) studied the conceptual learning and research possibilities: Bruner's view. The study centres round concept learning, which is the most important part of the academic discipline. Concepts acquired with understanding serve as tools not only for acquisition of new concepts but also for solving problems. Major findings were (i) one common characteristic feature running across all the definitions given was that there was an abstraction process in which similarities in objects were stressed and differences in them were ignored, (ii) the Concept Attainment Model (CAM) was more effective than the conventional method for the teaching of concepts, especially at the knowledge and understanding levels, for retention of concepts, and for bringing about attitudinal changes. [HLS 1499]

Khan, Mohd. Sharif and Siddiqui, Mujibul Hassan. (1992) studied the effectiveness of concept-attainment strategies. In methodology, the author reviewed the studies conducted earlier in India and abroad on concept attainment strategies at different levels. After classifying them into two broad categories, i.e., selection strategies and reception strategies, the author also touched upon their effectiveness for learning. Major findings were (i) all concepts possessed at least four components: attributes, examples, definitions and hierarchical relations, (ii) the factors that effected the selection strategies and reception strategies to attain concepts were definition of task; nature of the instances encountered; nature of validation; anticipating consequences of categorising; and nature of imposed restrictions, (iii) the concept attainment strategies were more effective over the traditional approach in teaching, (iv) personality factors had no significant effect on the concept attainment process, (v) disjunctive concepts were significantly more difficult than the attainment of conjunctive concepts, and (vi) concept attainment strategies were responsive to the needs of the disadvantaged learners in problem-solving situations and attainment of concepts. [MPR 1896]

Mohanty, B.K. (1992) studied the relative effectiveness of using the Jurisprudential Inquiry Model and the Concept Attainment Model in the cognitive development in moral-judgement, moral-concepts and personal-values of secondary school students. The study addresses the problem of the relative effectiveness of using the Jurisprudential Inquiry Model and the Concept Attainment Model in the cognitive development in moral-judgement, moral-concepts and personal-values of secondary school students. In methodology, the sample of the study consisted of 290 children of class VIII belonging to four high school of Baripada in the district of Mayurbhanj. Among four high schools, two boys' high school and two girls' high schools were taken for conducting the experiment. The tools used included group test of Mental Ability by Jalota, Socio-economic Status Scale of Bharadwaj, Gupta and Chauhan, Defining Issue Test (DIT) by Mohanty, Moral Concept Development Test (MCDT) by Mohanty and Personal Value Questionnaire (PVQ) of Sherry and Verma. Mean, SD, 't' test and correlation were used to treat the data. Major findings were (i) JIM was effective for the development of moral judgement of students but not the Concept Attainment Model (CAM), (ii) JIM was a better treatment than CAM for development of moral judgment of students, (iii) CAM produced better effect on the development of moral concept of students than JIM, (iv) social and health values developed through CAM, but religious, democratic, aesthetic, economic, knowledge, hedonistic power and family prestige values did not, (v) JIM was more effective on the development of social, economic, knowledge and power value than CAM, but there was no significant difference in the effects of the two treatments on other values, (vi) the relationship between moral judgement and values like social, democratic, aesthetic, knowledge, power and health was significant and positive. But there existed a negative and significant relationship between moral judgment and economic and between moral judgment and family prestige values, (vii) JIM was effective for the development of moral judgement of boys and girls, (viii) CAM produced greater effect on the development of moral judgment of girls than of boys, (ix) there was no difference in the development of moral concepts among boys and girls on JIM treatment, (x) CAM was more effective for the development of the moral concepts of boys than of girls, (xi) there was a significant and positive relationship between MCDT scores and SES scores, and (xii) the partial correlation between intelligence and MCDT scores, after partialling out DIT scores, was found to be positive and significant. [KCP 0447]

Anuradha Joshi and Anand Patra (1993) conducted an experiment to study the impact of the Concept Attainment Model (CAM) on general mental ability of secondary school social science students. Ten concepts of economics were taught to both the groups pre-test-post-test control group design was adopted. Major findings were (i) the adjusted mean General Mental Ability Scores of the student taught through CAM was significantly different from those taught through Traditional Method when pre-general mental ability scores were taken as covariate, (ii) the adjusted mean mental ability scores of the students taught through CAM boys significantly higher than those taught through TM.

Patil, Smita Ashok (1995) made a comparative study of the effectiveness of Inductive Thinking Model and Concept Attainment Model for teaching Marathi Grammar to Class VII students.

Ayishabi , T. C. (1996) made an experimental study of teaching of zoology though CAM at the +2 level. The study with the post exposure design was conducted on 40 students, each of the experimental and control group to compare the effect of CAM and traditional teaching method in ten selected topics of zoology at the +2 level. The finding showed no difference in the attainment of concept in the selected topics between the experimental and control groups overall boys, girls and experimental and control groups equated for intelligence.

Kaur, R. P. and Kaur Harvinder (2000) studied the effectiveness of Concept Attainment Model for teaching of concepts in economics in class XI.

Bairagya, S.S., Ghosh, S.K and Mete, J. (2005) studied on Relative Effectiveness between Concept Attainment Model and Traditional

Method of Teaching in Economics. Objectives were: (i) to teach a unit on prices in economics through CAM and TMT to two groups respectively; (ii) to compare the achievement levels of the learning groups, CAM and TMT; and (iii) to compare the outcomes of CAM and TMT with respect to attainment of Knowledge, understanding, application levels of learning. Major findings were: (i) the experimental group (CAM) achieved a significantly higher mean score compared to the mean test score of control group (TMT). This reveals that the CAM was comparatively effective teaching treatment than the TMT in teaching Economics at the HS level. (ii) the two learning groups did not differ with respect to the knowledge level learning objective. But the CAM was found to be more effective than TMT in respect to the 'Understanding' and 'Application' levels of learning objectives. The study indicates that the CAM is found to be more effective than the TMT in Economics particularly in respect to the higher order learning of the cognitive domain of the students.

2.1.1 RESEARCH STUDIES ABROAD OF CONCEPT ATTAINMENT MODEL

Lemke (1965) found that the verbal comprehension factor was related to the task factors, which suggested that inclusion of additional factors from its domain might account for additional variance in the study of abilities and their relationships to concept attainment and information processing.

Mascole (1967) found that significantly greater performance was demonstrated by groups having a course organised around the key conceptual schemes as compared to groups having a course not so organised.

Carol (1968) found a significant relationship between cognitive level and performance, the formal group performed more efficiently that the concrete group.

Kornriech (1969) found significantly more students in the guided discovery group acquired the strategy than in the other two groups.

Klausimier and Davis (1970) found that individuals identified as highly analytic solved the concept identification problem with greater ease than that did low analytic subjects.

Wager (1972) found the significant of different sequencing strategies on concept attainment.

Peters (1973) found significant difference between the good and poor readers who used the Test-book-Approach.

Balley (1974) found that the canonical teaching procedure was adequate for permitting attainment of the specified instructional objectives.

Benton (1977) found a significant difference between the mean gain scores for two attribute concepts and three attribute concepts.

Charles (1978) found that the use of non-examples may facilitate the acquisition of certain mathematical concepts.

Jolly (1978) found that laboratory approach was as effective as lecture discussion method for teaching the concept to average seventh grade students.

Miller (1980) found that the result of the study were inconsistence with Bruner's theory of cognitive growth.

Fulton (1981) found that there were a significant mean scores differences between the control group and method 'A' the science concept test.

Bernt (1986) found that current models of problem solving and hypothesis testing among young school children, methodological issues surrendering the use of the concept identification paradigms as means of studying children's cognitive skills were also considered.

Dalton (1986) found that teachers using these two strategies (Concept Attainment and Synectics) reported nearly twice as many thoughts related to both objectives and instructional procedures.

Oeballas (1986) found that for the age group of fourth graders, inductive and deductive approaches are equally effective in promoting concept formation/concept attainment and in fostering the metacognitive strategies that are crucial to higher-order thinking.

Al-Sulman (1987) found on significant difference to exist in the measure of an understanding of longitude and the causes of the changes of the seasons. A significance difference was obtained for the category of attributes. Concept attainment was most directly impacted by the parent's educational background and the degree of mobility experienced by the students.

Morrison, G. R., Ross, S. M., and Kemp, J. E. (2001) designed effective instruction based on the terminal objective of the instruction; concept learning and assessment can focus on both recall and application of the to-be-learned concept.

Jonassen, D., Strobel, J., and Gottdenker, J. (2005) studied on model building for conceptual change. Interactive Learning Environments, some view model building as an ideal practice and guidance strategy for concept learning as models require learners to externalise their understanding of not only the concept, but also conceptual relationships.

Jonassen, D. (2006) studied on the Role of Concepts in Learning and Instructional Design, argued that the historical focus of concept learning has been on concept attainment as a discrete and terminal learning outcome without regard to where the concept fits within a larger conceptual framework. In contrast, Jonassen suggested a focus on concepts-in-use in which concept learning centers on concepts as mental model building blocks. As such, Jonassen argues that the instruction and assessment should shift beyond the learner's ability to identify, discriminate, and generalise membership based on concept attributes and examples to how the learned concepts are organised within the learner's overall conceptual framework. He asserts that concept learning and assessment should focus on the learner's ability to describe or represent conceptual patterns and propositions, as in concept maps, word associations, and model building.

2.1.2 AN OVERVIEW OF RESEARCH STUDIES OF CONCEPT ATTAINMENT MODEL

There were different strategies of concept attainment like reception, selection and sequencing, etc., which showed significant effect on the efficiency of learning performance of the students in the research studies of Lemke, Elmer Allen, (1965), Mascole, Rechard Peter (1967), Carol, Keller, (1968), Kornriech, I.B. (1969), Klausimier and Davis (1970), Wager (1972), Peters, Charles Warren, (1973), Bally, Harald J. (1974), Benton, E.R. (1977), Rottavina, Charles, R.L. (1978), Jolly, E.D. (1978), Miller, R. (1980), Fulton, Anne Ware, (1981), Antimadas (1986), Bernt, F.M. (1986), Dalton, Machaelleon, (1986), Pani, Pushpanjali (1986), Oeballas, Elva Guajardo, (1986), Bihari, S.K. (1986), Al-Sulman (1987), Pillai, A.S. (1989), Bawa, M.S. (1991), Khan, Mohd. Sharif and Siddiqui, Mujibul Hassan. (1992), Mohanty, B.K. (1992), Joshi, Anuradha and Patra, Anand (1993), Patil, Smita Ashok (1995), Ayishabi, T.C. (1996), Kaur, R.P. and Kaur Harvinder (2000), Morrison, G. R., Ross, S. M., & Kemp, J. E. (2001), Bairagya, S.S., Ghosh, S.K and Mete, J. (2005), Jonassen, D., Strobel, J., & Gottdenker, J. (2005), Jonassen, D. (2006).

2.2.0 RESEARCH STUDIES IN INDIA OF ADVANCE ORGANISER MODEL

Panda (1986) determined the effect of Advance Organiser Model on learning from text material of ninth grade pupils, the effect of Advance Organiser Model and TraditionalMethod of teaching on the achievement of ninth grade pupils; and influence interactiobetween methods of instruction, sex and criterion test. The sample consisted of 60 students of St. Marry High School of Indore. He found that the difference between the mean achievement of pupils studying through Advance Organiser Model set induction and Traditional Method were significant.

Senapati (1986) compared Programmed Learning Material, Advance Organiser Material and Traditional Method in terms of achievement of students studying through them; and studied the personality factors and their interaction with the treatment on achievement of students. Sample consisted of 139 student-teachers in the Development of Education in D.A.V., Indore. The Advance Organiser Materials were more effective than both the Programmed Learning Material and Traditional Method in terms of achievement of students on criterion test. The personality factors did not influence the achievement of students on criterion test.

Rajoria (1987) studied the effectiveness of Advance Organiser Model and the Traditional Method. The sample consisted of 114 student of Class VIII in Government Middle School No. 24, Indore. She found that the Advance Organiser Model was significantly superior to Traditional Method in terms of achievement in science of Class VIII students when the groups were matched separately in respect of intelligence and previous year achievement in science.

Gupta, Suman. (1991) studied the effectiveness of the Advance Organiser Model of Ausubel in developing the teaching competence of student-teachers, and their attitude towards teaching. This is an experimental study and the researcher has assessed the effectiveness of Ausubel's model in developing teaching competence. Objectives were (i) to compare the effectiveness of teaching through the Advance Organiser Model (AOM) of Ausubel and the conventional method in the simulated condition in development of the teaching competence of student-teachers, (ii) to compare the effectiveness of teaching through the AOM of Ausubel and the conventional method in real classroom conditions in development of the teaching competence of student-teachers, and (iii) compare the effect of teaching through AOM and the conventional method on the attitude of student-teachers towards teaching. In methodology, the sample comprised 100 B.Ed. students of the 1985-86 session from Bijnor and Dhampur teachers' training colleges, who had offered Hindi as one of the teaching subjects. The purposive sample procedure was followed. The tools used included Teacher Attitude Inventory of S. P. Ahluwalia, Teaching Competency Scale of NCERT, and Model Assessment Guide. Mean, SD and "t" test were used to treat the data. Major findings were (i) there existed a significant difference in the teaching competence between the experimental and the control groups of student-teachers. The effect of training on the AOM approach on the experimental group was visible as they had high teaching competence in the simulated condition, (ii) there existed a significant difference in the teaching competence between the experimental and control groups. It was Indicated that the experimental group was better after using the AOM of Ausubel so far as teaching competence was concerned in the real classroom situation, and (iii) there existed a significant difference in the attitude of the experimental and control groups and student-teachers. There was the effect of the AOM approach on the attitude of the experimental group of student-teachers. [SS 0794]

Panda (1994) Studied the effect of advance organiser and set induction on learning and transfer among class IX students.

Jadhav Vandana Vishnu (2008) studied the effectiveness of Advance Organiser Model on Student – Teachers' Teaching and its Influence on the School Pupil's Performance in Science. Objectives were (i) to develop self- instructional material on theory, planning and evaluation of AOM suitable for Indian conditions, (ii) to analyse the Science Syllabus of Std. IX to identify the units, which can be taught using AOM, (iii) to determine the Student Teachers' teaching performance using AOM and (iv) to determine the student teachers' performance in terms of achievement of pupils in paper-pencil tests based on different sub units in Science. Major findings were (i) the final draft of the self-instructional material was found comprehensive, self explanatory and instructive for planning and practice teaching, (ii) out of the syllabus prescribed for Std. IX, 75 sub-units were found suitable to the Advance Organiser Model (AOM), (iii) in the first two lessons the teaching performance of the conventional group was found comparatively effective in simulated situation, whereas, in the last three lessons the teaching performance of AOM and conventional groups was found equally effective in simulated conditions, (iv) the AOM group of student teachers was found more effective than conventional method group in real classroom situations and (v) the performance of AOM group of student teachers was found superior in terms of pupils' achievement than that of the conventional group. It is an interesting and appealing study. The research rigor has been observed throughout the study. The study has very well demonstrated the effectiveness of the Advance Organiser Model at Teacher Education and School Education, both, the levels. The study has contributed significantly to the knowledge base in the area of Educational Technology, particularly, Models of Teaching.

2.2.1 RESEARCH STUDIES ABROAD OF ADVANCE ORGANISER MODEL

Ausubel (1960) found the significant difference between means of experimental and control groups at 0.01 level in favour of the group using the expository advance organiser.

Ausubel and Fitzgerald (1962) found significant results for the lower one-third group in favour of the expository organiser (PL.01).

Scandura and Wells (1967) found that the advance organiser was superior to the historical introduction.

Weisberg (1969) found a significant difference between map as graph organisers and verbal advance organiser.

Smith (1976) found that advance organisers seemed to have effect on long range retention.

Derr (1978) found that students who had either behavioural objectives or sample tests as advance organisers did better on post-test then students who had no organisers, comparison of cell means indicated that sample tests were more effective organisers than objectives.

Meena, Victor George (1979) found that both written and graphic advance organiser treatment were significantly superior to non-organiser treatment.

Darrow (1980) found that advance organiser and the conventional overview treatments were equally effective for both measures.

Lali (1980) found that advance organisers significantly increased performance on teacher made test.

Lemke (1980) found that the programmed instruction seemed to provide more effective learning than that taking place through use of a study guide using advance organisers as an ancillary method of instruction.

Martin (1980) found that the usage of comparative organisers improved retention of the theoretical concept of the study.

Giles (1981) found that one teacher utilising different mediators of learning can bring about significantly different learning outcomes.

Haghighi (1981) found that both advance organiser and underlined cues facilitated meaningful prose learning.

Brune (1982) found that advance organisers facilitated listening comprehension for both learning disabled and non-learning disabled groups in both narrative and expository modes. The non-learning disabled group scored significantly higher than the learning disabled group when advance organiser used.

Rodman (1982) found that it is possible that organisers have their strongest impact in situations requiring transfer of previously learned material.

Lenz (1983) found that advance organisers can exert a positive qualitative influence on the learning disabled adolescents.

Mahajan (1983) found a significant interaction between the cognitive level and the absence or presence of organisers.

Miller (1984) found that the visual organiser group scored significantly better on immediately recall than the control group.

Cliburn (1985) found that experimental group scores on the delayed post-test were significantly higher than those of the control group.

Morgan (1985) found facilitating effects of advance organisers on both student achievement and student attitudes.

Lasky (1986) found that advance organisers were an effective instructional strategy with bilingual learning disabled students.

Puhan, G., and Hu, H. (2006) in their study also found that motivation is an important predicator of science achievement than gender.

Prokop, P., Tuncer, G. and Chuda, J. (2007) also posit that teacher characteristics have a significant role on students' attitude towards biology. Perhaps this would also explain the gender differences in motivation noted in this study. This also seems to suggest that more research needs to be devoted to the role of teacher characteristics on students' motivation to learn science.

Hudson Shihusa and Fred N. Keraro (2009) studied on Advance Organisers to Enhance Students' Motivation in Learning Biology. Major findings of this study have shown that advance organisers enhance learners' motivation to learn. The use of advance organisers in this study, therefore, enabled learners to be active cognitively and hence was motivated to learn biology.

2.2.2 AN OVERVIEW OF RESEARCH STUDIES OF ADVANCE ORGANISER MODEL

Advance Organiser Model had significant effect on active learning, achievement and retention situation positively to traditional method and these effects were found in the research studies of Ausubel, D.P. (1960), Ausubel, David P. and Fitzgeald, D. (1962), Scandura, J.M. and Well, H.N. (1967), Weisberg, Joseph Simpson (1969), Smith, C.D. (1976), Derr, K.T. (1978), Meena, V.G. (1979), Darrow, Donald Richard (1980), Lalli, E.D. (1980), Lemke, W.R. (1980), Martin, D.A. (1980), Giles, T. W. (1981), Haghighi, F. (1981), Brune, Patrica Anne (1982), Rodman, S.M. (1982), Lenz, B.K. (1983), Mahajan, Sharmila Roy (1983), Miller, Ronald, E. (1984), Cliburn, J.W. (1985), Morgan, Barbara Small (1985), Lasky, Beth Anne (1986), Panda, Bibhutibhusan (1986), Senapati, Sanjukta (1986), Rajoriya, (Miss) Renuka (1987), Kaushik, Gupta, Suman. (1991), Panda, B.B. (1994), Puhan, G., and Hu, H. (2006), Prokop, P., Tuncer, G. and Chuda, J. (2007), Jadhav Vandana Vishnu. (2008), Hudson Shihusa and Fred N. Keraro. (2009).

2.3.0 RESEARCH STUDIES OF BOTH CONCEPT ATTAINMENT MODEL AND ADVANCE ORGANISER MODEL

Jamini, N. (1991) studied the relative effectiveness of Advance Organiser Model (AOM) and Concept Attainment Model (CAM) on conceptual learning efficacy and retention of chemistry concepts in relation to divergent thinking indicated that although both AOM and CAM were equally effective in fostering concept learning, the AOM was comparatively more beneficial in concept learning to pupils with divergent thinking, while CAM was more beneficial to pupils with low divergent thinking. The AOM was found to be more effective than CAM in the retention of concepts irrespective of the level of divergent thinking of the pupils.

Kaur, Rajinder Pal. (1991) studied effectiveness of the Bruner and the Ausubel models for teaching of concepts in economics to high and low achieving students across creativity levels. The study attempts to compare the effectiveness of the Bruner and Ausubel models for teaching concepts of economics to students having different levels of achievement and creativity. Objectives were (i) to determine the teaching effectiveness of Bruner's Concept Attainment Model, Ausubel's Advance Organiser Model and conventional teaching in the teaching of concepts economics in relation to the various levels of academic achievement and creativity of students, (ii) to compare the teaching effectiveness of Bruner's Concept Attainment Model and Ausubel's Advance Organiser Model, (iii) to compare Bruner's Concept Attainment Model and the conventional method of teaching, (iv) to compare Ausubel's Advance Oganiser Model and the conventional method of the teaching, and, (v) to have these three comparisons in relation to different levels of academic achievement and creativity. Major findings were (i) the results of one-way ANCOVA revealed a statistically significant difference between students who had been taught through Bruner's Concept Attainment Model, Ausubel's Advance Oganiser Model and conventional teaching with respect to the scores on attainment of concept in economics; also Ausubel's Advance Organiser Model was more effective than conventional teaching; further Ausubel's Advance Organiser Model was more effective than conventional teaching, whereas no statistically significant difference was found in the effectiveness of the two experimental groups. (ii) while applying three-way ANOVA (3 X 2 X 2) to gain scores in concept learning in economics among 120 students, a statistically significant difference was found between the three teaching approaches were Ausubel's Advance Organiser Model was found to be more effective than Bruner's Model; Bruner's Model was more effective than the conventional method and Ausubel's model was more effective than the conventional method, (iii) neither academic achievement nor creativity affected the gain scores of subjects pertaining to the attainment of concepts in economics, (iv) the interactions between teaching approaches and academic achievement, between teaching approaches and creativity, and between academic achievement and creativity were not significant, and (v) the interaction between teaching approaches, intelligence and creativity was not significant. [AK 1853]

Mahajan, Jyotsna. (1992) compared the effectiveness of two models of teaching, viz. Bruner's Concept Attainment Model and Ausubel's Advance Organiser Model, on the teaching abilities of student-teachers and on achievement of students in various schools. This is a study Wherein the method of teaching is tested against the teaching abilities of student-teachers in junior college of education. It work in two phases: Phase A - college-based laboratory phase; Phase B - school-based coaching phase. Objectives were (i) to enable student-teachers to be familiar with various steps involved in models of teaching, (ii) to enable student-teachers to use the teaching-analysis guide to observe lessons, (iii) to enable student-teachers to write the lesson notes according to the mode and to teacher in peer group, and (iv) to enable student-teachers to plan a complete unit in mathematics for a longer period and to teach accordingly in the classroom situation. In methodology, a pilot study was conducted to validate the programmes, namely lesson notes and other teaching material, based on the two models. On the basis of the scores on the Teaching Competence Scales and the uniform criterion for evaluation of teaching practices, three groups were formed; namely, High (H), Middle (M) and Low (L). Each group consisted of 15 student-teachers. Three treatments were assigned to 9 sub-group of H, M and L groups. All other factors were controlled. The experiment was conducted for two months for phase A, and for one month for Phase B. The tools used were Teaching Competence Assessment Scale, Uniform Criterion for Evaluating Teaching Practice, and Achievement Test for students. The data were analysed using ANOVA. For further comparisons between the multiple means, Schelt's test was used. Major findings were (i) during the peer-group sessions as well as classroom teaching sessions, the group which was taught by the Concept Attainment Model based on Bruner's theory was found to be superior to the group which was taught by the Advance Organiser Model based on Ausubel's theory and the group which was taught by the routine method, so far as the teaching ability of the student-teacher was concerned, (ii) the achievement of students who were taught by the Concept Attainment Model based Bruner's theory were found to be better than those of the students taught by Ausubel's Advance Organiser Model and the routine Method. [AGB 1288]

Ghosh, S. and Mukhopadhyaya, D. (2004) studied the effectiveness of Information Processing Model over Traditional Teaching Methods for Teaching English as Second Language in Secondary Schools. Objective was to compare and determine experimentally, the relative effectiveness of Information Processing Model (IPM) over Traditional Teaching Method (TTM) for teaching English as second language (L2) in secondary schools in West Bengal. Major findings were significant difference was found between the achievement scores of the two groups. The Experimental Group taught through IPM did much better than Control group.

Sidhu, R.K. and Singh, P. (2005) evaluated the comparative study of Concept Attainment Model, Advance Organiser Model and Conventional Method in Teaching of Physics in Relation to Intelligence and Achievement Motivation of Class IX Students. Objectives were (i) to study the effect of Bruner's Concept Attainment Model on scholastic achievement as compared to conventional method of teaching in Physics in relation to intelligence and achievement motivation; (ii) to study the effect of Ausubel's Advance Organiser Model on scholastic achievement as compared to conventional method of teaching in physics in relation to intelligence and achievement motivation; and (iii) to study the relative effectiveness of Bruner's Concept Attainment Model and Ausbel's Advance Organiser Model on scholastic achievement in Physics in relation to intelligence and achievement motivation. In methodology, the sample consisted of 240 students of Class IX, enrolled in Government Senior Secondary School, Kanganwal; Government High School, Jhuner, and Government Senior Secondary School, Sandaur (Dist. Sangrur, Punjab) divided into three groups (n=80 each), two experimental groups and one control group. Pre-test, Post-test control group quasi-experimental design was employed. The statistical technique of three way analysis of variance (3×2×2) was used on gain scores for finding out the main effect and interaction effect of teaching techniques, intelligence and achievement motivation on scholastic achievement in physics of Class IX students. The experiment was conducted in three stages–pre-test treatment and post-test in all the three groups. Meenakshi's Socio-economic Status Scale, Jalota's Verbal Group test of General Mental Ability, Achievement Motivation test of Pratibha Deo and Asha Mohan, Lesson plans and a criterion test in physics were used for the study. Major finding was (i) there was no significant effect between various teaching techniques, intelligence and achievement motivation on scholastic achievement of students for learning of concepts in physics.

2.3.1 AN OVERVIEW OF RESEARCH STUDIES OF BOTH CONCEPT ATTAINMENT MODEL AND ADVANCE ORGANISER MODEL

Some of the research studies indicated equal effect of Concept Attainment Model and Advance Organiser Model over Traditional Method. These effects were found in the research studies of Jamini, N. (1991), Kaur, Rajinder Pal. (1991), Mahajan, Jyotsna. (1992), Ghosh, S. and Mukhopadhyaya, D. (2004), Sidhu, R.K. and Singh, P. (2005).

2.4.0 IMPLICATION OF PREVIOUS RESEARCH FOR THE PRESENT STUDY

From the above discussion on the review of related studies it was found that no such studies have been undertaken by the researchers considering two independent variables like Concept Attainment Model and Advance Organiser Model and two dependent variables like concept development and achievement in teaching science at primary level. So, the present research study is a new one and has significance for the learner, learning process and teacher.

3.0.0 INTRODUCTION

O nce the research problem is formulated unambigiously and plan of the research is clearly specified, the next problem is to build up a research design to streamline the research. A research design is a string of logic that ultimately links the data to be collected and the conclusions to be drawn to the initial questions of the study. In other words, it is a master plan specifying the methods of conducting research and what methods to be used. According to Best and Khan (1986), "Scientific problem can be resolved only on the basis of data and a major responsibility of a scientist is to setup a research design capable of providing data necessary to the solution of his problem. Collection of data is of paramount importance in the conduct of research." In any educational research, 'Methodology' plays a very crucial role as it provides substantial logic and logistics to the procedure and progressed of a research so that it can proceed towards the designed goal.

The present experimental study entitled as *"A study of effectiveness of Concept Attainment Model and Advance Organiser Model in the development of concept and achievement in science of primary school students"*. In the first chapter the needs, objectives and hypothesis of the study have been discussed. In the second chapter, the review of the related literature has been presented. The present chapter is devoted to the methodology adopted in the study. The methodology is discussed under the following main captions.

1. Sample
2. Variables used
3. Design of the study
4. Tools used
5. Procedure of data collection
6. Statistical analysis.

3.1.0 SAMPLE OF THE STUDY

Most of the educational phenomenon consist of a large number of units. The larger group about which the generalisation is made is called population and the small group that is observed is called a sample. Sampling is indispensable to the researcher. Usually, the time, money and effort involved, do not permit a research to study all possible number of a population. Furthermore, it is generally not necessary to study all possible cases to understand the phenomenon under consideration. Hence, sampling, helps to select a relatively small number of individuals or objects or events which are the representative of the entire population.

Sampling procedure provides generalisation on the basic of a relatively small portion of the population. Usually it involves the following steps:

1. Defining and listing the population.
2. Selecting a representative sample.
3. Obtaining an adequate sample.

In the study, district, block, school and class were selected on the basis of "purposive sampling". Only class IV was selected purposively. The sample of the study consisted of 107 students of class - IV belonging to four primary schools in the district of Mayurbhanj, Odisha. Among the four primary schools, two primary schools were taken as Experimental Groups and other two schools were taken as Control Groups for conducting the research. These four schools are co-educational and had sufficient facilities for the experimental study. In the present investigation two types of treatments were used. The first treatment was "Concept Attainment Model" (CAM) and the second one was "Advance Organiser Model" (AOM). From four schools, two schools were taken as Experimental Group - I and Experimental Group - II and other two schools were taken as Control Group - I and Control Group - II.

The sample of the study was 107 students of class IV belonging to four co-educational schools. From those schools, Sanachatra Nodal Primary School was selected to the first teaching strategy - Concept Attainment Model (CAM) and taken as Experimental Group - I (Ex1), Budhikhamari Primary School was selected to the other teaching strategy - Advance Organiser Model (AOM) and taken as Experimental Group - II (Ex2), and out of the rest schools, Badachatra Primary School was selected as Control Group - I (C1) and Bhugudakata Primary School was selected as Control Group - II (C2), which were received the Traditional Method. The first Experimental Group was consist of 35 students, out of them24 were boys and 11 were girls. This Experimental Group was received the treatment of 'Concept Attainment Model'. The Control Group - I, which received the treatment of the 'Traditional Teaching Method' provided by the school teacher of the concerned subject, was consist of 17 students out of which 7 were boys and 10 were girls. Similarly, another Experimental Group was received the treatment of 'Advance Organiser Model', which was consist of 34 students. Out of which, 13 were boys and 21 were girls. The Control Group - II was also received the treatment of the 'Traditional Teaching Method' provided by the school teacher of the concerned subject, which was consist of 21 students out of which, 11 were boys and 10 were girls.

3.2.0   VARIABLES USED

(A) Independent variables:
The present study took into consideration the following independent variables:

1. Sex	:	Male and Female
2. Class	:	IV
3. Subject	:	Science
4. Teaching Method	:	(i) Concept Attainment Model
		(ii) Advance Organiser Model

(B) Dependent variables:

1. Concept Development in Science
2. Achievement in Science

3.3.0   DESIGN OF THE STUDY

Kerlinger (1973) defined research design as "the plan, structure and strategy of investigation conceived so as to obtain answers to research questions and control variance". The plan includes an outline of what the investigator will do from writing the hypothesis to the final analysis of the data. The structure refers to scheme of the operation of variables. The strategy implies how the research objectives will be reached. Shulman (1970) suggested a scheme for examining the variables which should be considered in formulating propositions about the best form of instruction, particularly when the practitioner is confronted with a contrasting array of positions. Since Concept Attainment Model (CAM) and Advance Organiser Model (AOM) of teaching involved in the present study took contrasting position with respect to attainment of educational objectives, the choice of variables for this study was done according to the Shulman scheme. The type of instructions was Bruner's Concept Attainment Model and Ausubel's Advance Organiser Model.

The present study was experimental in design. In this study, it was necessary to use "Two groups - pre-test - post-test - parallel group design". The main focus of the present study was to make a study of the effectiveness of the Concept Attainment Model and Advance Organiser Model over Traditional Method, i.e. to make a comparative study of the effectiveness of two models of teaching over Traditional Method of teaching. For this purpose, there is the requirement of two Experimental Groups and two Control Groups. The first teaching strategy was Concept Attainment Model and the second one was Advance Organiser Model. The Concept Attainment Model was developed by Bruner for better conceptualisation of the subject matter in the class room. And the second teaching model namely Advance Organiser Model was developed by David Ausubel which has great potential in teaching concepts, relationships, imparting and assimilating the information and ideas effectively and meaningfully. For this purpose four schools were selected for the study.

For conducting the experiment 30 lesson plans were prepared separately for each teaching strategy from unit II to IX of class IV science syllabus. The lesson plans were prepared according to the phases or steps of the each teaching strategy. These lesson plans were taught in both the experimental groups through the procedure of CAM and AOM teaching strategies. To measure

Intelligence of the students, an Intelligence test version by Dr. Rama Tiwari was translated into mother tongue Odia language. To measure the development of concepts and achievement of the students, a Concept Development Test in Science (CDTS) and an Achievement Test in Science (ATS) were developed and standardised by the investigator with the help of the guide. All these tests were also printed in the press. For administration of tests and teaching lessons, a time-table was prepared for each school after consulting with the concerned Headmasters.

After adequate preparation and planning, on the first day the Intelligence Test was administered on the students of each school. On the second day, the Concept Development Test in Science was administered in each school and on the third day, Achievement Test in Science also administered in each school. All the above three tests were administered as pre-tests in three successive days in each school. After the pre-tests were conducted in four schools, the experimental groups were taught by the investigator according to the treatments and the control groups were taught by the concerned school science teacher according to the Traditional Method. Each type of teaching strategy was imparted for thirty classes of 45 minutes for 10 weeks. Hence, both the experimental treatments were completed within ten weeks.

After the experimental treatments were imparted, the following post-tests were administered to all the experimental and control groups.

1) Concept Development Test in Science (CDTS)
2) Achievement Test in Science (ATS)

3.4.0 TOOLS USED

In order to draw any valid conclusion from an experimental research, tools used for the measurement of variables should be reliable and valid. This requirement is usually met by employing standardised tests. Since no research has been done in the area selected for the research, the researcher constructed her own test for the purpose. The present study required the following tools and measures.

1) Intelligence Test (IT)
2) Concept Development Test in Science (CDTS)
3) Achievement Test in Science (ATS)

3.4.1 INTELLIGENCE TEST

Intelligence Test or General Mental Ability Test (GMAT) was constructed and standardised by Dr. Rama Tiwari, Agra University, Agra; Published by Agra Psychological Research Cell (APRC). It is a test of verbal intelligence which consists of 70 questions. The included sub-tests are:

(i)   Classification or spotting the stranger.
(ii) Number series.
(iii) Analogy
(iv) Problem solving
(v) Choosing
(vi) Reasoning or logical solution
(vii) Numerical ability

To evaluate the student's intelligence level "General Mental Ability Test" (GMAT) already constructed and standardised for the pupils of age range from 13 to 18 years was administered on the sample which consisted of both 'Experimental Groups' and 'Control Groups' numbering 107 students including both boys and girls.

The test was a speed test comprising seventy (70) test items which were all multiple choice type questions. Each question carries equal weightage of one (1) mark. So the full mark was 70 and the allotted time was 20 minutes. As the standardised question paper on 'General Mental Ability Test' was originally constructed in English, it was translated in to Odia by the investigator to suit age, ability and comprehension of the students whose mother tongue is Odia. With the co-operation of the heads of the institutions and teachers of science subject of the respective schools, the said test was administered smoothly. The classroom environment was favourable and the psychological condition of the students was normal and stable.

The reliability of the test had been calculated by Kuder Richarson formula number 20 and "Split half Method". The co-relation coefficient came to 0.87 and 0.92 respectively which was very high.

3.4.2 CONCEPT DEVELOPMENT TEST

The Concept Development Test was constructed by the investigator. It included the test items which were framed according to the following behavioural objectives:

1. Knowledge
2. Understanding
3. Application
4. Skill

The test-items also covered the following units selected from the science text book of class - IV prescribed by the Orissa Board of Primary and Mass-education. The content areas also classified according to the different objectives to evaluate the various abilities of the students of class - IV.

Unit - II:	Our Food.
Unit - III:	Contaminated food and drinking water.
Unit - IV:	Purification of drinking water.
Unit - V:	Unhygienic places and diseases.
Unit - VI:	Functions of different parts of a plant.
Unit - VII:	Use of different plants and animals.
Unit - VIII:	Protection and care of animals and plants.
Unit - IX:	Harmful insects and unnecessary plants.

The development of the test items of the Concept Development Test were gradually developed according to the following steps:

3.4.2.1 DEVELOPMENT OF THE TEST ITEMS OF THE CONCEPT DEVELOPMENT TEST

i) The researcher selected the test items from the selected content area, keeping in mind the predetermined objectives. The researcher took help of the concept of bloom's "Taxonomy of Objectives" and prepared a large number of test items (100 test items) at the initial stage. The test items were made on the basis of knowledge, understanding and application. At this stage, objective type of test items was made.

ii) Instructions regarding the ways of giving answers to the question were written in clear and unambiguous language or words.

iii) Each question carried one mark only. Initially there were 50 positive examples and 50 negative examples.

3.4.2.2 OPINION OF RESOURCE PERSONS ON THE TEST ITEMS

All the test items in the manuscripts were placed before respected, well-versed experts to seek their valuable opinions for modification. With their opinions, necessary correction, addition and alteration of the questions, if and where necessary, were made.

3.4.2.3 TRYOUT OF THE TEST ITEMS

Before the final selection of the test, tryout is essential. The objectives of the try out were:

i) To estimate the difficulty index of each item.
ii) To estimate the discriminating power of each item.
iii) To finalise the number of item to be included in the final test.
iv) To incorporate necessary modifications, if any in the text.

So, for this, the following steps were undertaken by the researcher.

(a) Selection of the sample

A sample of 50 students belongs to different sexes and strata of the society were selected. i.e.25 boys and girls from urban areas and 25 boys and girls from suburban areas respectively from Baripada Municipality.

(b) Administration of the test for tryout

The test was administered on the sample in a congenial environment.

A considerable time was allowed to enable them to respond all the questions comfortably. At the tryout stage the time limit was generous. The time taken by individual student was recorded and the average time taken by the student was 40 minutes.

(c) Evaluation of the answer scripts

The scoring was made according to the scoring key already prepared by the investigator. Each correct answer was credited with full marks and wrong answer was awarded zero (0).

(d) Item analysis

For item analysis, the following steps were taken by the investigator.

i) First, the answer scripts of 50 students were arranged in order of their size of the test score. i.e. from the highest to the lowest score.
ii) Following the suggestion of Kelley (1939), the upper 27% and lower 27% of the examinees were selected and the middle 46% were laid aside.
iii) For each item, the number of examinees of the upper group who gave correct answer was counted. It was RU.
iv) For each time, the number of examinees of the lower group who gave correct answers was counted. It was RL.
v) Then the following formula was followed to find the difficulty value of each test item.

$$\text{Difficult level} = \frac{RU+RL}{NU+NL} \times 100$$

Ru = No. of examinee of the upper group who gave correct answer.

RI = No. of examinees of the lower group who gave correct answer.

Nu = No. of examinees of the upper group.

Nl = No. of examinees of the lower group.

The investigator classified the test items according to difficulty value such as:

Extremely difficult (0% - 20%), difficult (21% - 40%), average (41% - 60%), easy (61% - 80%), extremely easy (81% - 100%).

(vi) To find out the discriminating value of the test items, the investigator used the following formula:

$$\text{Discriminating value} = \frac{RU-RL}{1/2T}$$

T = Total no. of examinees

3.4.2.4 FINAL SELECTION OF THE TEST ITEMS FOR CONCEPT DEVELOPMENT TEST

For the final selection of the test items for the Concept Development Test, the following procedures were followed:

i) The test items which were extremely easy or difficult were discarded.

ii) The test items which had "Discriminative value" zero (0) or negative index was discarded as well.

iii) Garret (1962, P - 368) suggests that items with validity indices of 0.20 or more are regarded as satisfactory. So, the test items which had "Discriminative value" 0.20 or more were selected. According to Taiwo, A. A (1995, P - 60), the test items possessing difficulty indices between 30% and 70% were satisfactory for practical purpose. In all, 20% of the easy, 60% of the average and 20% of the difficult test items were selected for the final test.

iv) Taiwo, A. A. (1995, P - 60) observes that the test items possessing difficulty indices between 30% and 70% are satisfactory for practical purpose. Keeping this in mind, the test item was mostly selected from the above range. 20% of easy, 60% of average and 20% of the difficult test items were selected for the final test.

v) As a result, the full marks of final test items were reduced to 50 and the time determined for test was 40 minutes.

According to the result of analysis, out of 100 items which were included in the tryout form of the test, only 50 items were retained and 50 items were rejected because they could not yield satisfactory discriminating index. Out of selected 50 test items, 25 were positive examples and 25 were negative examples.

3.4.2.5 REPRESENTATION OF THE DESIGN AND BLUE PRINT FOR THE FINAL SELECTION OF THE TEST ITEMS OF THE CONCEPT DEVELOPMENT TEST

(a) Objectives

Sub - Science	Full marks - 50
Class - IV	Time-40 minutes

Behavioural Objectives:

After the completion of the test, the student will be able to -

(i) Judge the types of food according to their nutritious values.

(ii) Know about the classification of food.

(iii) Know about the functions of different nutrients.

(iv) Recognise the ways through which the drinking water get contaminated.

(v) Recognise the ways through which food get contaminated.

(vi) Know about the procedures of purification of drinking water.

(vii) Find out the difference between the clean and contaminated water.

(viii) Know about the demerits of unhygienic.

(ix) Identify the causes of diseases.

(x) Know about the functions of different parts of plants.

(xi) Acquire knowledge about deforestation and afforestation.

(xii) Find out the causes of deforestation and the impact on our day to day life.

(xiii) Recognise the importance of afforestation in the present situation.

(xiv) Acquire knowledge about the uses of different plants and animals.

(xv) Acquire knowledge about the medical values of plants.

(xvi) Know about the uses of different animals in our day to day life.

(xvii) Acquire knowledge about how to give protection to the plants and animals.

(xviii) Know the procedures of taking care of different plants and animals.

(xix) Acquire knowledge about the National parks.

(xx) Know about the harmful characteristics of insects and plants.

(b) Design in terms of weightage to different components of the Concept Development Test

Table - 3.1
Weightage to Objectives

Objectives		Weightage
(i)	Knowledge	20(40%)
(ii)	Understanding	20(40%)
(iii)	Application	10(20%)
		50(10%)

Table - 3.2
Weightage to Content

	Contents	Weightage
(ii)	Our food.	5 (10%)
(iii)	Contaminated food and water.	5 (10%)
(iv)	Purification of drinking water.	4 (8%)
(v)	Unhygienic places and diseases.	8 (16%)
(vi)	The functions of different parts of plants.	9 (18%)
(vii)	Use of different plants and animals.	10 (20%)
(viii)	Protection and care of plants and animals.	6 (12%)
(ix)	Harmful insects and plants.	3 (6%)
		50 (100%)

Table - 3.3
Weightage to Test Items

	Types of test items	Weightage
	Objective type	
(i)	Positive Examples	25 (50%)
(ii)	Negative Examples	25 (50%)
		50 (100%)

Table - 3.4
Weightage to difficulty level

	Test item	Weightage
(i)	Easy	10 (20%)
(ii)	Average	30 (60%)
(iii)	Difficult	10 (20%)
		50 (100%)

Table – 3.5
Blueprint of Concept Development Test

Objective	Knowledge			Understanding			Application			
Content	S. A	V. S. A	O	S. A	V. S. A	O	S. A	V. S. A	O	TOTAL
Our food.			2(2)			2(2)			1(1)	5(5)
Contaminated food and drinking water			2(2)			2(2)			1(1)	5(5)
Purification of drinking water.			2(2)			1(1)			1(1)	4(4)
Unhygienic places and diseases.			4(4)			2(2)				8(8)
The functions of different parts of plants.			3(3)			5(5)			1(1)	9(9)
Use of different plants and animals.			3(3)			5(5)			2(2)	10(10)
Protection and care of plants and animals.			3(3)			2(2)			1(1)	5(5)
Harmful insects and plants.			1(1)			1(1)			1(1)	3(3)
Total			20(20)			20(20)			10(10)	50

The figures outside the brackets indicate - 'Marks'.
The figures inside the brackets indicate - 'The no. of question'.

3.4.2.6 CONSTRUCTION OF THE FINAL CONCEPT DEVELOPMENT TEST

(i) The researcher selected the test items from the selected areas, keeping in mind the predetermine objectives.

(ii) Instructions regarding giving answers to questions were written in clear and unambiguous words.

(iv) Marks were individually allotted to the question according to the difficult levels. Both marks and difficulty - levels were determined according to the judgement, experience and insight of the researcher. The maximum mark is 50. The time limit for the test is 40 minutes.

3.4.2.7 DEVELOPMENT OF THE SCORING KEY

The scoring key was developed by the researcher to ensure uniformity and objectivity in assessment and making scheme. Each correct answer was awarded one (1) mark and the wrong answer was awarded zero (0).

3.4.2.8 RELIABILITY OF THE FINAL CONCEPT DEVELOPMENT TEST

The final test composed of the selected test item was administered on a fresh sample of 40 students of class - IV, randomly selected from an urban and a Suburban primary schools which were also randomly selected from a list of primary schools located at Baripada in the district of Mayurbhanj. After completion of the administration of the final test, the answer scripts were evaluated by the investigator with the help of the scoring key.

After 15 days from the date of administration of the final test the same test was readministrated on the same group. To reduce the memory effect to a minimum level, the re-test was taken after 15 days as mentioned before. The environmental conditions were kept constant on two occasions to reduce the psychological variation.

After the test re-test method the reliability of the test was determined by "Product Moment Method". The correlation co-efficient between the test and re-test was found to be 0.91, which showed a high positive correlation. Thus the reliability of the test was assured.

3.4.2.9 VALIDITY OF THE FINAL CONCEPT DEVELOPMENT TEST

According to Garret, there are two ways to determine the validity of an instrument -

(i) Determining validity by means of judgment, i.e. (content validity and face validity.)

(ii) Determining validity experimentally, i.e. (criterion related validity and index of reliability). Stanley, J. and Koul, Lokesh emphasise only on content validity in measurement of validity of an Achievement Test. However, to ensure the validity, the investigator took a great care to construct the test.

a) Face validity - In the present study, a good number of experts were engaged to assist the investigator in the preparation of the test. The test was said to have face validity as the test items looked valid to them.

b) Content validity - The content area of the test was analysed in terms of objectives. The final test was developed on the basis of specification tables and blue print.

c) Item validity - The discriminating index was prepared for all the items by item analysis and those items having high discriminating power were retained in the final test.

d) Intrinsic validity - The high positive reliability co-efficient of the answer its intrinsic validity.

Thus the validity of the test was assured.

3.4.2.10   OBJECTIVITY OF THE TEST

a) Objectivity in construction - In the present study the test items were impartially selected on the basis of specification tables and blue print.

b) Objectivity in administration - The test and re-test method was adopted in administration of the test on the sample of students randomly selected from different sexes and status. During administration both the environmental and psychological conditions were controlled as far as possible.

c) Objectivity in scoring - In the present study a scoring key was development to ensure uniform, impersonal and unbiased evaluation of the answer scripts.

Thus, the objectivity of the test was assured.

The Concept Development Test was thus prepared by the investigator to assess the development of science concepts of class - IV students. The test contained 50 concepts selected from the class - IV science text book. Each item in the final test was either positive or negative example of the concept. On the right hand of the each test item, there are two spaces for giving answers. The first space is for 'positive'(+) and the second space is for 'negative' (-) examples. Students were directed to read the statement of each concept and tick off the space below (+) if the answer is right and the space below (-) if it is wrong. Each correct answer to the positive or negative type of example carries one mark, the maximum marks was 50 and the time limit was 40 minutes.

3.4.3 ACHIEVEMENT TEST

The Achievement Test constructed by the investigator includes the test items which were framed according to the following behavioural objectives:

1. Knowledge
2. Understanding
3. Application
4. Skill

The test item also covered the following science units selected from the text book of Science prescribed by Orissa Board of Primary and mass-education. The content areas also classified according to different objectives to evaluate various abilities of the student of class - IV.

1. Our food.
2. Contaminated food and drinking water.
3. Purification of drinking water.
4. Unhygienic places and diseases.
5. The functions of different parts of plants.
6. Use of different plants and animals.
7. Protection and care of plants and animals.
8. Harmful insects and plants.

The development of the test items of the Achievement Test were gradually developed according to the following steps:

3.4.3.1 DEVELOPMENT OF THE TEST ITEMS OF THE ACHIEVEMENT TEST

i) The researcher selected the test item from the selected content areas, keeping in mind the predetermined objectives. The researcher took help of the concepts of the bloom's "Taxonomy of Objectives" and prepared a large number of test items (100 test items) at the initial stage. The test items were made on the basis of knowledge, understanding, application and skills.

ii) Instructions regarding the ways of giving answers to the question were written in clear and unambiguous language or words.

iii) Mark was individually allotted to the question according to the difficulty level. Both marks and difficulty level were determined according to the judgement, experience and insight of the researcher.

3.4.3.2 OPINION OF RESOURCE PERSONS ON THE TEST ITEMS

All the test items in the manuscripts were placed before respected, well-versed experts to seek their valuable opinions for modification. With their opinions, necessary corrections, addition and alteration of the questions, if and where necessary, were made.

3.4.3.3 TRYOUT OF THE TEST ITEMS

Before the final selection of the test, tryout is essential - The objectives of the tryout were:

i)   To estimate the difficulty index of each item.
ii) To estimate the discriminating power of each item.
iii) To finalise the number of items to be included in the final test.
iv) To incorporate necessary modifications, if any, in the text.

So, for this, the following steps were undertaken by the researcher.

a) Selection of the sample
A sample of 40 students belonging to different sexes and strata of the society was randomly selected i.e. 20 boys and girls from urban areas and 20 boys and girls from suburban areas.

b) Administration of the test for tryout
The test was administered on the sample in a congenial environment on the second day, just after the day of administration of the Concept Development Test as a tryout.
A Considerable time was allowed to enable them to respond all the questions
comfortably. At the tryout stage the time limit was generous. The time taken by individual student was recorded and the average time taken by the students was 40 minutes.

c) Evaluation of the answer scripts

The scoring was made according to the scoring key already prepared by the investigator. Each correct answer was credited with full marks. A fully incorrect answer was awarded zero (0).

d) Item - Analysis

For item - analysis, the following steps were taken by the investigator:

i) First, the answer scripts of 40 (forty) students were arranged in order of their size of the test score i.e. from the highest to lowest score.
ii) Following the suggestion of Kelly (1939), the upper 27% and lower 27% of the examinees were selected and the middle 46% were laid aside.
iii) For each item, the number of examinees of the upper group who gave correct answer was counted. It was RU.
iv) For each item, the number of examinees of the lower group who gave correct answer was counted. It was RL.
v) Then the following formula was followed to find out the difficult level of each test item.

$$\text{Difficult level} = \frac{RU+RL}{NU+NL} \times 100$$

RU = No. of examinees of the upper group who gave right answer.
RL = No. of examinees of the lower group who gave right answer.
NU = No. of examinees of the upper group.
NL = No. of examinees of the lower group.

The investigator classified the test items according to difficulty value such as: extremely difficulty (0% - 20%), difficult (21% - 40%), average (41% - 60%), easy (61% - 80%), extremely easy (81% - 100%).

vi) To find out the discriminating value of the test items, the investigator used the following formula:

$$\text{Discriminating value} = \frac{RU-RL}{1/2T}$$

T = Total No. of examinees.

3.4.3.4 FINAL SELECTION OF THE TEST ITEMS FOR ACHIEVEMENT TEST

For final selection of the test items for the Achievement Test, the following procedures were followed:

i) The test items which are extremely or very easy or difficult were discarded.
ii) The test items which have "discriminative value" zero (0) or negative index were discarded as well.
iii) The test items which had "discriminative value" 0.20 or more were selected.
iv) The test items possessing difficulty indices between 30% and 70% were also selected. In all, 20% of the easy, 60% of the average, 20% of the difficult test items were selected.
v) As a result, the full marks of final test items were reduced to 40 and the time determined for the test was 40 minutes.

So, according to the results of analyses, out of 100 item which are included in the tryout form of the test, only 40 items are retained and 60 items were rejected because they could not yield satisfactory discriminating index.

3.4.3.5 REPRESENTATION OF THE DESIGN AND BLUE PRINT FOR THE FINAL SELECTION OF THE TEST ITEMS OF THE ACHIEVEMENT TEST

(a) Objectives

Sub - Science   Full Marks - 40
Class- IV   Time-40 minutes

Behavioural objectives:

After the completion of science test, the students will be able to -

(i)   Acquire knowledge about the types of nutrients exist in food.
(ii) Acquire knowledge about the functions of carbohydrate, fat, protein, vitamin and mineral.
(iii) Identify the causes due to which food and drinking water get contaminated.
(iv) Identify the diseases occurring due to contaminated food and drinking water.
(v)   Find out the procedures to purify drinking water.
(vi) Differentiate between saturate and unsaturated things.
(vii) Find out the causes of deforestation and the impact on our day to day life.
(viii) Recognise the importance of afforestation in the present situation.
(ix) Acquire knowledge about how to give protection to the plants and animals.
(x)   Know the procedures of taking care of different plants and animals.
(xi) Acquire knowledge about the National parks.
(xii) Know about the harmful characteristics of insects and plants.

(b) Design in terms of weightage to different components of the Achievement Test

Table – 3.6
weightage to objectives

	Objectives	Weightage
(i)	Knowledge	10(25%)
(ii)	Understanding	10(25%)
(iii)	Application	10(25%)
(iv)	Skill	10(25%)
		40(100%)

Table – 3.7
Weightage to Content

	Contents	Weightage
(ii)	Our food.	8 (20%)
(iii)	Contaminated food and water.	3 (7.5%)
(iv)	Purification of drinking water.	4 (10%)
(v)	Unhygienic places and diseases.	6 (15%)
(vi)	The functions of different parts of plants.	8 (20%)
(vii)	Use of different plants and animals.	7 (17.5%)
(viii)	Protection and care of plants and animals.	1 (2.5%)
(ix)	Harmful insects and plants.	3 (7.5%)
		40 (100%)

Table – 3.8
Weightage to Test Items

Type of test items		Weightage
Objective type		
(i)	Fill in the blanks	10 (25%)
(ii)	Multiple choice	10 (25%)
(iii)	Completion type	10 (25%)
(iv)	Find out the odd one	5 (12.5%)
(v)	Matching	5 (12.5%)
		40 (100%)

Table – 3.9
Weightage to difficulty level

Test items		Weightage
(i)	Easy	10 (20%)
(ii)	Average	20 (60%)
(iii)	Difficult	10 (20%)
		40 (100%)

Table – 3.10
Blueprint of Achievement Test

Objective	Knowledge			Understanding			Application			Skill			
Content	S. A	V. S. A	O	S. A	V. S. A	O	S. A	V. S. A	O	S. A	V. S. A	O	TOTAL
Our food.			2(2)			2(2)			2(2)			2(2)	8(8)
Contaminated food and drinking water			1(1)			---			1(1)			1(1)	3(3)
Purification of drinking water.			1(1)			1(1)			1(1)			1(1)	4(4)
Unhygienic places and diseases.			1(1)			3(3)			1(1)			1(1)	6(6)
The functions of different parts of plants.			2(2)			3(3)			2(2)			1(1)	8(8)
Use of different plants and animals.			2(2)			---			2(2)			3(3)	7(7)
Protection and care of plants and animals.			---			---			1(1)			---	1(1)
Harmful insects and plants.			1(1)			1(1)			---			1(1)	3(3)
Total			10(10)			10(10)			10(10)			10(10)	40

The figures outside the brackets indicate - 'Marks'.
The figures inside the brackets indicate - 'The no. of question'.

3.4.3.6 CONSTRUCTION OF THE FINAL ACHIEVEMENT TEST

(i)   The researcher selected the test-items from the selected areas, keeping in mind the predetermine objectives.

(ii) Instructions regarding giving answers to question were written in clear and unambiguous terms or words.

(iii) Marks was individually allotted to the question according to the difficult level of the question. Both marks and difficulty level were determined according to the judgement, experience and insight of the researcher. The maximum mark is 40. The time limit for the test is 40 minutes.

3.4.3.7 DEVELOPMENT OF THE SCORING KEY

The scoring key was developed by the researcher to ensure uniformity and objectivity in assessment and marking scheme. Each correct answer was awarded one (1) mark and the wrong answer was awarded zero (0).

3.4.3.8 RELIABILITY OF THE FINAL ACHIEVEMENT TEST

The final test composed of the selected test item was administered on a fresh sample of 40 students of class - IV, randomly selected from an urban and a suburban primary schools which were also randomly selected from a list of primary schools located at Baripada in the district of Mayurbhanj. After completion of the administration of the final test, the answer scripts were evaluated by the investigator with the help of the scoring key.

After 15 days from the date of administration of the final test the same test was re-administered on the same group. To reduce the memory effect to a minimum level, the re-test was taken after 15 days as mentioned before. The environmental conditions were kept constant on two occasions to reduce the psychological variation.

After the test re-test method, the reliability of the test was determined by "Product Moment Method". The correlation co-efficient between the test and re-test was found to be 0.93, which showed a high positive correlation. Thus the reliability of the test was assured.

3.4.3.9 VALIDITY OF THE FINAL ACHIEVEMENT TEST

According to Garret (2005, P. 356 - 357) there are two approaches in determining the validity of an instruments. (i) Determining validity by means of judgement (content validity and face validity). (ii) Determine validity experimentally (criterion related validity and index of reliability). To ensure the validity, the investigator took a great care to construct the test. Due attention was paid to maintain the following types of validity of the instrument.

a) *Face Validity:* In the present study, a good number of experts were engaged to assist the investigator in the preparation of the test. The test was said to have face validity as the test items looked valid to them.

b) *Content Validity:* The content area of the test was analysed in terms of objectives. The final test was developed on the basis of specification tables and blueprints.

c) *Item Validity:* The discriminating index was prepared for all the items by item-analysis and those items having high discriminating power were retained in the final test.

d) *Intrinsic Validity:* The intrinsic validity is maintained by determining the reliability of the instrument. Accordingly, the high positive reliability co-efficient of the test assured the Intrinsic Validity of the test. Thus, the validity of the test was maintained.

3.4.3.10 OBJECTIVITY OF THE TEST

a) Objectivity of the construction: In the present study the items were impartially selected on the basis of specification tables and blueprint.

b) Objectivity in administration: The test and re-test method was adopted in administration of the test on the sample of 107 students randomly selected from different sexes and strata. During administration both the environmental and psychological conditions were controlled as far as possible.

c) Objectivity in scoring: In the present study, a scoring key was developed to ensure uniform, impartial and unbiased evaluation of the answer scripts. Thus, the objectivity of the test was assured.

3.5.0. PROCEDURE OF DATA COLLECTION

After construction and standardisation of Concept Development Test and Achievement Test, the investigator made proper planning for administration of the Intelligence Test along with the Concept Development Test and Achievement Test on the sample of 107 students selected from four co-educational Primary schools of Baripada to carry out her study. The Headmasters and concerned teachers were contacted and with their consent a time-schedule was prepared for administration of these 3 tests as pre-tests. As stated before, all students of four schools of class-IV were included in the sample. The following tests were administered before the treatment as pre-tests.

1. Intelligence Test (Standardised)
2. Concept Development Test on Science
   (Constructed by the investigator)
3. Achievement Test on Science
   (Constructed by the investigator)

After the treatment was over, the same Concept Development Test and the Achievement Test were re-administered on the same students as post-tests.

1. Concept Development Test on Science
2. Achievement Test on Science

After the completion of these tests, the answer scripts were examined by the investigator. The scores in these tests were the only data used in the study.

3.6.0 STATISTICAL ANALYSIS

After scoring the test, Mean (M), Standard Deviation (SD) of the scores were obtained. Significance of difference between means scores of different groups as well as of the same groups in the pre-tests and post-tests were determined and the co-efficient of correlation was calculated between scores of different variables to find the nature of relation if any between them.

4.0.0   INTRODUCTION

The data of the study has been presented in the previous chapter. The methodology followed in this study has been explained in the third chapter.

The objectives along with the hypotheses have been stated in the first chapter.

The present chapter is devoted to the analysis of data and the interpretation of results. The results have been interpreted with respect to the objectives stated in Chapter one.

4.1.0   EFFECTIVENESS OF CONCEPT ATTAINMENT MODEL IN THE DEVELOPMENT OF CONCEPTS.

The first objective of the present investigation is "to study the effectiveness of Concept Attainment Model in the development of concepts of primary students in science". The hypothesis corresponding to this objective is that "there is no significant difference in the Mean Concept Development Test Gain Scores of Experimental Group – I and Control Group - I". Keeping this hypothesis in mind the Concept Development Test Gain Scores data were analysed with the help of "t" test between Experimental Group - I and Control Group - I. The results are given in table - 4.1.

Table – 4.1

"t" test between mean Concept Development Test Gain Scores of Experimental Group - I and Control Group - I.

Group	Mean CDT Gain Scores	SD	N	"t" value	Result
Ex_1	24.76	3.02	35	22.95	Significant at 0.01 level
C_1	9.84	1.72	17		

Significant at 0.01 level

$df = n_1 + n_2 - 2 = 35 + 17 - 2 = 50$

From the table - 4.1, it is observed that the "t" value 22.95 is significant at 0.01 level for df equal to 50. It indicates that the mean Concept Development Test Gain Scores of Experimental Group - I and Control Group - I differ significantly from each other. In other words, the Concept Attainment Model produced different effect on the development of scientific concepts of students. So, the null hypothesis "there is no significant difference in the Mean Concept Development Test Gain Scores of Experimental Group - I and Control Group – I" is rejected. Further the mean gain scores of Experimental Group – I and Control Group - I were 24.76 and 9.84 respectively. It reflects that the treatment Concept Attainment Model provided to the students of Experimental Group - I have significantly positive effect on the development of concepts of students in science. So, it was concluded that the treatment Concept Attainment Model is effective for developing scientific concepts of students.

DISCUSSION

The result revealed that the Concept Attainment Model is effective in the development of scientific concepts of primary school students. The Concept Attainment Model was used in the Experimental Group by the investigator and the Traditional Method was used by the subject teacher in the Control Group. The same contents from science text book of class - IV from Unit – II to IX were taught to both the groups. The result indicated that there was significant difference between the mean gain scores of Experimental and Control Groups and the mean gain scores of the Experimental Group is much higher than the Control Group. In other words, the treatment Concept Attainment Model which was applied in the Experimental Group is more effective than the Traditional Method. The investigator found that the Concept Attainment Model is effective in comparison to Traditional Method of teaching. The reason for the effectiveness of the model lies in its lesson-plans, which were constructed in a logical, sequential and systematic process.

Basically, in the Concept Attainment Model, the investigator has followed three essential phases. In the first phase, the investigator presented an array of examples (positive) and non-examples (negative). The examples were labeled as 'yes' and the non-examples as 'no' and were presented one by one. At each encounter, the learners compared the attributes in positive and negative instances and formulated and reformulated hypotheses with regard to the concepts. Then the students were asked to name the concepts and state the rules or definitions of the concepts according to their essential attributes. The investigator extended support to the students in case students find any difficulty in naming the concepts or stating the rule. In phase two, an array of unlabelled examples was presented and the students were asked to label them as 'yes' or 'no'. To ensure complete learning thereafter, the students were asked to give a few examples of the concepts on their own. In phase three, the students were asked to analyse the strategies that they had followed to attain the concepts. By following the phases of this model, it had been observed that the Concept Attainment Model is very appropriate, systematic, organised, scientific approach which helped the students to develop the understanding of the facts and information effectively and also helped the students for better conceptualisation of the subject matter of science of class – IV, but these steps and techniques were not followed by the subject teacher in the Control Group. Hence, the result has been found that the Concept Attainment Model is effective in comparison to Traditional Method in the development of concepts in science of class – IV students.

4.2.0 EFFECTIVENESS OF CONCEPT ATTAINMENT MODEL IN THE ACHIEVEMENT OF STUDENTS.

The second objective of the study is "to study the effectiveness of Concept Attainment Model in the achievement of primary students in science." The hypothesis corresponding to this objective is that "there is no significant difference in the Mean Achievement Test Gain Scores of Experimental Group – I and Control Group – I". Keeping this hypothesis in mind, the Achievement Test Gain Scores data were analysed with the help of "t" test between Experimental Group - I and Control Group - I. The results are given in the table – 4.2.

Table - 4.2

"t" test between Mean Achievement Test Gain Scores of Experimental Group - I and Control Group - I

Group	Mean AT Gain Scores	SD	N	"t" value	Result
Ex_1	20.60	2.66	35	22.38	Significant at 0.01 level
C_1	6.50	1.81	17		

Significant at 0.01 levels
$df = n_1 + n_2 - 2 = 35 + 17 - 2 = 50$

From the Table - 4.2, it was observed that the "t" value 22.38 is significant at 0.01 level for df equal to 50. It indicates that the Mean Achievement Test Gain Scores of the Experimental Group - I and Control Group - I differ significantly from each other. In other words, the treatment Concept Attainment Model produced differential effect on the achievement of students in science, so the null hypothesis "there is no significant difference between the Mean Achievement Test Gain Scores of Experimental Group - I and Control Group - I" is rejected. Further, the mean gain scores of Experimental Group - I and Control Group - I were 20.60 and 6.50 respectively. It reflects that the treatment Concept Attainment Model provided to the students of Experimental Group - I has significant positive effects in the achievement of students. So it was concluded that the treatment Concept Attainment Model is effective for achievement of students in science.

DISCUSSION

The result revealed that the effectiveness of Concept Attainment Model regarding the achievement of students in science is higher than the Traditional Method. The Concept Attainment Model was used in the Experimental Group by the investigator and the Traditional Method was used by the subject teacher in the Control Group. The same contents from science test book of class – IV from unit - II to IX were taught in both the groups. After the analysis of data, we came to know that there was significant difference in the mean gain scores between the Experimental Group - I and the Control Group - I and the mean gain scores of Experimental Group is higher than the Control Group. In other words, the treatment Concept Attainment Model applied in the Experimental Group was more effective than the Traditional Method, regarding the achievement of students in science.

Hence, we came to know that Concept Attainment Model is more effective teaching strategy than Traditional Method regarding the achievement of class - IV students in science because in this strategy, the students remain attentive to learn and attain the concepts easily as they get themselves involved in the environment of active teaching-learning process. As far as the Concept Attainment Model is concerned, the emphasis is given more to cognitive development and from the theories of learning, it is clear that the cognitive development facilitates more learning and achievement of the students. The most important aim of this model is to acquaint the students with the pre-existing concepts. The researcher was able to do the task. The researcher presented the materials before the students through the model was so organised that the students were able to acquire the concepts easily, due to which the level of achievement taught through Concept Attainment Model was higher than the achievement level of students taught through the Traditional Method. But, in the Traditional Method the subject teacher did not followed any such procedures or lesson-plans. Hence, the result has been found that the Concept Attainment Model is effective in comparison to Traditional Method in the achievement of class – IV students in science.

4.3.0   EFFECTIVENESS OF ADVANCE ORGANISER MODEL IN THE DEVELOPMENT OF CONCEPTS.

The third objective of the study is "to study the effectiveness of Advance Organiser Model in the development of concepts of primary students in science". The hypothesis corresponding to this objective is that "there is no significant difference in the mean Concept Development Test Gain Scores of Experimental Group - II and Control Group - II" keeping this hypothesis in mind the Concept Development Test Gain Scores data were analysed with the help of "t" test between Experimental Group - II and Control Group – II. The results are given in the table – 4.3.

Table - 4.3

"t" test between Mean Concept Development Test Gain Scores of Experimental Groups - II and Control Group – II.

Group	Mean CDT Gain Scores	SD	N	"t" value	Result
Ex_2	22.27	5.53	34	12.70	Significant at 0.01 level
C_2	9.06	2.11	21		

Significant at 0.01 level
$df = n_1 + n_2 - 2 = 34 + 21 - 2 = 53$

From the table 4.3, it is observed that the "t" value 12.70 is significant at 0.01 level with df equal to 53. It indicates that the Mean Concept Development Test Gain Scores of the Experimental Group - II and Control Group - II differ significantly from each other. In other words, the treatment Advance Organiser Model produced differential effect in the development of concepts of primary students. So, the null hypothesis "there is no significant difference in the Mean Concept Development Test Gain Scores of Experimental Group - II and Control Group - II" is rejected. Further the mean gain scores of Experimental Group - II and Control Group - II were 22.27 and 9.06 respectively. It reflects that the treatment Advance Organiser Model provided to the students of Experimental Group - II has significant effect on the development of concepts of the primary students. So, it was concluded that the treatment Advance Organiser Model is effective for developing concepts of students than the Traditional Method.

DISCUSSION

The result revealed that the Advance Organiser Model is effective in the development of scientific concepts of primary school students. The Advance Organiser Model was used in the Experimental Group by the investigator and the Traditional Method was used by the subject teacher in the Control Group. The same contents from unit - II to IX from the science text book of class - IV were taught in both the groups. The result indicated that there is significant difference in the mean gain scores of Experimental Group and Control Group. The Mean Concept Development Test Gain Scores of Experimental Group is higher than the Control Group. In other words, the treatment Advance Organiser Model applied in the Experimental Group is more effective than the Traditional Method.

From the above discussion, we came to know that, the Advance Organiser Model is effective than the Traditional Method in the development of concepts. The reason of effectiveness of the treatment of Advance Organiser Model lies in its certain steps, which has been followed for teaching science lessons in the present study. In the first step, the advance organiser was presented. This step consists of three activities: clarifying the aims of the lesson, presenting the advance organiser and promoting awareness of relevant knowledge. In step two, the learning task or material was presented. In this phase an important task is to maintain student's attention. Another task is to make the organisation of the learning material explicit to the students, so that they had an overall sense of direction. Further more, the logical order of the material was to be made explicit so that the students could see how the ideas relate to each other. In the last step, the new learning material was anchored in the students existing cognitive structure. This phase consists of four activities: promoting integrative reconciliation, promoting active reception learning, eliciting a principle approach to subject matter and clarification of the subject matter. Hence, it has been realised that due to follow these phases or steps, this model has great potential in teaching concepts, relationships and imparting information effectively. Just opposite to the treatment, in the Control Group, the subject teacher did not follow these steps and techniques through the Traditional Method. Hence the Advance Organiser Model is more effective than the Traditional Method in teaching science to primary students.

4.4.0 EFFECTIVENESS OF ADVANCE ORGANISER MODEL IN THE ACHIEVEMENT OF STUDENTS.

The fourth objective of the present investigation is "to study the effectiveness of Advance Organiser Model in the achievement of primary students in science". The hypothesis corresponding to this objective is stated that "there is no significant difference in the Mean Achievement Test Gain Scores of Experimental Group - II and Control Group - II". Keeping this hypothesis in mind the Mean Achievement Test Gain Scores were analysed with the help of "t" test between Experimental Group - II and Control Group - II. The results are given in the table - 4.4.

Table - 4.4

"t" test between Mean Achievement Test Gain Scores of Experiment Group - II and Control Group – II.

Group	Mean AT Gain Scores	SD	N	"t" value	Result
Ex_2	20.84	1.99	34	24.88	Significant at 0.01 level
C_2	6.16	2.28	21		

Significant at 0.01 level
$df = n_1 + n_2 - 2 = 34 + 21 - 2 = 53$

From the table 4.4, it was observed that the "t" value 24.88 is significant at 0.01 level for df equal to 53. It indicated that the Mean Achievement Test Gain Scores of Experimental Group - II and Control Group - II differ significantly from each other. In other words, the treatment Advance Organiser Model produced differential effect on the achievement of students. So, the null hypothesis "there is no significant difference in the Mean Achievement Test Gain Scores of Experimental Group - II and Control Group – II" is rejected. Further the Mean Achievement Test Gain Scores of Experimental Group - II and Control Group – II were 20.84 and 6.16 respectively. It reflects that the treatment Advance Organiser Model provided to the students of Experimental Group - II has significant effect on the achievement of students. So, it was concluded that the treatment Advance Organiser Model is effective for development of achievement of primary students.

DISCUSSION

The result revealed that the Advance Organiser Model is effective on the achievement of primary school students. The Advance Organiser

Model was used in the Experimental Group by the investigator and the Traditional Method was used by the subject teacher in the Control Group. The same contents from unit - II to IX from the science text book of class - IV were taught in both the groups. The result indicated that there is significant difference in the Mean Achievement Gain Scores of Experimental Group and Control Group. Hence, the mean gain scores of Experimental Group is higher than the Control Group. In other words, the treatment Advance Organiser Model applied in the Experimental Group is more effective than the Traditional Method.

As far as the effectiveness of Advance Organiser Model is concerned, it is derived from the theory of meaningful verbal learning to facilitate the learning and achievement level. If a particular learner possesses ideas in his cognitive structure to which the new learning material can be related in a substantive and non-arbitrary fashion, then we can say that the material is potentially meaningful to him, or that it possesses potential meaningfulness. On the basis of this few theoretical aspect of Advance Organiser Model propounded by David. P. Ausubel, the researcher developed her lesson plans, so that, the students could understand the learning materials which were presented in systematic, meaningful and logical way. But in the Traditional Method, the subject teacher did not follow such steps and techniques in his teaching learning process, due to which the achievement of primary students of Experimental Group - II was higher than the achievement of students of Control Group - II. This fact shows that the Advance Organiser Model is superior or effective than the Traditional Method in the achievement of primary students in science.

4.5.0 COMPARATIVE EFFECTIVENESS OF CONCEPT ATTAINMENT MODEL AND ADVANCE ORGANISER MODEL IN THE DEVELOPMENT OF CONCEPTS.

The fifth objective of the present investigation is "to study the comparative effectiveness of Concept Attainment Model and Advance

Organiser Model in the development of concepts of primary students in science". The hypothesis corresponding to this objective is that "there is no significant difference in the Mean Concept Development Test Gain Scores between Experimental Group - I and Experimental Group - II taught thought Concept Attainment Model and Advance Organiser Model respectively". Keeping this hypothesis in mind the Mean Concept Development Test Gain Scores data were analysed with the help of "t" test between Experimental Group – I and Experimental Group - II. The results are given in the table - 4.5.

Table - 4.5

"t" test between Mean Concept Development Test Gain Scores of Experimental Group - I and Experimental Group – II.

Group	Mean CDT Gain Scores	SD	N	"t" Value	Result
Ex_1	24.76	3.02	35	2.32	Significant at 0.01 level
Ex_2	22.27	5.53	34		

Significant at 0.01 level.
df = $n_1 + n_2 - 2 = 35 + 34 - 2 = 67$

From the table - 4.5, it was observed that the "t" value 2.32 is significant at 0.01 level for df equal to 67, it indicates that the Mean Concept Development Test Gain Scores of Experimental Group - I and Experimental Group - II differ significantly from each other. So, the null hypothesis "there is no significant difference in the Mean Concept Development Test Gain Scores of both Experimental Group - I and Experimental Group - II" is rejected. Further the Mean Concept Development Test Gain Scores of Experiment Group - I and Experimental Group - II were 24.76 and 22.27 respectively. So, it was concluded that the treatment Concept Attainment Model is effective for the development of concepts of primary students in science than the treatment Advance Organiser Model.

DISCUSSION

The result revealed that the Concept Attainment Model is more effective than the Advance Organiser Model in the development of concepts of primary students in science. Both Concept Attainment Model and Advance Organiser Model were used in the Experimental Groups by the investigator. The same contents from unit - II to IX of the test book of science of class - IV were taught to both of the groups. The result indicated that there is significant difference in the Mean Concept Development Test Gain Scores of both Experimental Group - I and Experimental Group - II. Hence, the Mean Concept Development Test Gain Scores of Experimental Group - I is higher than the Experimental Group - II. In other words, the treatment Concept Attainment Model applied in the Experimental Group - I is more effective than the treatment Advance Organiser Model applied in the Experimental Group - II.

In the present study, it was found in the comparative effectiveness of both the models that the Concept Attainment Model was more effective for teaching scientific concepts to class - IV students than the Advance Organiser Model, so far as student's ability to acquire knowledge of the concepts were concerned. The main reason may be due to the development of lesson plans in a very systematic way which maximises the comprehension and understanding level of the students. From the above interpretation made by the researcher, it was concluded that Concept Attainment Model is better than Advance Organiser Model in the attainment of concepts.

4.6.0 COMPARATIVE EFFECTIVENESS OF CONCEPT ATTAINMENT MODEL AND ADVANCE ORGANISER MODEL IN THE ACHIEVEMENT.

The sixth objective of the present investigation is "to study the comparative effectiveness of Concept Attainment Model and Advance

Organiser Model in the achievement of primary students in science". The hypothesis corresponding to this objective is that "there is no significant difference in the Mean Achievement Test Scores between Experimental Group - I and Experimental Group – II". Keeping this hypothesis in mind the Achievement Test Gain Scores data were analysed with the help of "t" test between Experimental Group - I and Experimental Group - II. The results are given in the table 5.6.

Table - 4.6

"t" test between Mean Achievement Test Gain Scores of Experimental Group - I and Experimental Group - II.

Group	Mean CDT Gain Scores	SD	N	"t" Value	Result
Ex_1	20.60	2.66	35	0.43	Not Significant
Ex_2	20.84	1.99	34		

Not significant.

$df = n_1 + n_2 - 2 = 35 + 34 - 2 = 67$

From the table - 4.6, it was observed that the "t" value 0.43 is not significant for df equal to 67. It indicates that Mean Achievement Test Gain Scores of both Experimental Group – I and Experimental Group – II do not differ significantly from each other. So, the null hypothesis "there is no significant difference in the Mean Achievement Test Gain Scores between Experimental Group – I and Experimental Group – II" is not rejected. Further, the Mean Achievement Test Gain Scores of Experimental Group - I and Experimental Group - II were 20.60 and 20.84 respectively. So, it was concluded that the Mean Achievement Test Gain Scores of Experimental Group – I and Experimental Group - II do not differ significantly from each other and both the treatments Concept Attainment Model and Advance Organiser Model are equally effective for the development of achievement in science.

Dr. Sasmita Mohanty

DISCUSSION

The result revealed that both Concept Attainment Model and Advance Organiser Model are equally effective on the development of achievement of primary school students. Both Concept Attainment Model and Advance Organiser Model were used in the Experimental Groups by the investigator. The same contents from Unit - II to IX from the text book of science of class - IV were taught to both the groups. The result indicated that the mean gain scores of Concept Attainment Model and Advance Organiser Model do not differ significantly from each other. The reason may be that the steps and techniques followed in Concept Attainment Model and Advance Organiser Model were equally effective for the development of primary students in science.

In the present study, it was found that in the comparative effectiveness of Concept Attainment Model and Advance Organiser Model that there is no significant difference in the achievement of students taught by both the models. They have equal effect on students in terms of their achievement. The main reason for this may be due to the investigator developing the lesson plans based on both the strategies in a very systematic, logical and meaningful way.

4.7.0 DIFFERENCE IN THE CONCEPT DEVELOPMENT IN BOYS AND GIRLS TAUGHT THROUGH CONCEPT ATTAINMENT MODEL.

The seventh objective of the present investigation is "to find out the difference in the concept development in boys and girls taught through Concept Attainment Model". The hypothesis corresponding to this objective is that "there is no significant difference in Mean Concept Development Test Gain Scores between boys and girls taught through Concept Attainment Model". Keeping this hypothesis in mind the Mean Concept Development Test Gain Scores of boys and girls were analysed with the help of "t" test. The results are given in table – 4.7.

Table - 4.7

"t" test in Mean Concept Development Test Gain Scores between Boys and Girls.

Group	Mean CDT Gain Scores	SD	N	"t" value	Result
Boys	24.86	2.85	24	0.10	Not significant
Girls	25.00	4.00	11		

Not Significant

df = $n_1 + n_2 - 2$ = 24 + 11 - 2 = 33

From the table 4.7, it was observed that the "t" value 0.10 is not significant for df equal to 33. It indicates that the Mean Concept Development Test Gain Scores between boys and girls do not differ significantly from each other. So, the null hypothesis "there is no significant difference in the Mean Concept Development Test Gain Scores between boys and girls taught through Concept Attainment Model" is not rejected. Further, the mean gain scores of boys and girls were 24.86 and 25.00 respectively. So, it may be concluded that the treatment Concept Attainment Model is equally effective for the development of concepts of both boys and girls in science.

DISCUSSION

The steps and techniques followed in Concept Attainment Model are equally effective for both boys and girls in the development of concepts in science.

4.8.0 DIFFERENCE IN ACHIEVEMENT BETWEEN BOYS AND GIRLS TAUGHT THROUGH CONCEPT ATTAINMENT MODEL

The eighth objective of this study is "to find out the difference in the achievement between boys and girls taught through Concept Attainment Model". The hypothesis corresponding to this objective is that "there is no significant difference in the Mean Achievement Test Gain Scores of boys and girls taught through Concept Attainment Model". Keeping this hypothesis in mind the Mean Achievement Test Gain Scores of boys and girls were analysed with the help of "t" test. The results are given in table - 5.8.

Table - 4.8

"t" test in Mean Achievement Test Gain Scores between Boys and Girls.

Group	Mean CDT Gain Scores	SD	N	"t" Value	Result
Boys	20.58	2.24	24		
				0.35	Not Significant
Girls	20.22	3.07	11		

Not Significant

df = $n_1 + n_2 - 2$ = 24 + 11 - 2 = 33

From the table 4.8, it is observed that the "t" value 0.35 is not significant for df equal to 33. It indicates that the Mean Achievement Test Gain Scores between boys and girls do not differ significantly from each other. So, the null hypothesis "there is no significant difference in Mean Achievement Test Gain Scores of boys and girls taught through Concept Attainment Model" is not rejected. Further, the mean gain scores of boys and girls were 20.58 and 20.22 respectively. It may be concluded that the treatment Concept Attainment Model is equally effective for the development of achievement of boys and girls in science.

DISCUSSION

The steps and techniques followed in Concept Attainment Model are equally effective for both boys and girls in achievement in science.

4.9.0 DIFFERENCE IN THE CONCEPT DEVELOPMENT BETWEEN BOYS AND GIRLS TAUGHT THROUGH ADVANCE ORGANISER MODEL

The ninth objective is "to find out the difference in the concept development between boys and girls taught through Advance Organiser Model". The hypothesis corresponding to this objective is stated that "there is no significant difference in Mean Concept Development Test Gain Scores of boys and girls taught through Advance Organiser Model". Keeping this hypothesis in mind the Mean Concept Development Test Gain Scores were analysed with the help of "t" test between boys and girls. The results are given in table - 4.9.

Table - 4.9
"t" test in the Mean Concept Development Test Gain Scores of boys and girls.

Group	Mean CDT Gain Scores	SD	N	"t" Value	Result
Boys	22.07	6.67	13	0.08	Not Significant
Girls	21.88	5.84	21		

Not Significant
$df = n_1 + n_2 - 2 = 21 + 13 - 2 = 32$

From the table 4.9, it was observed that the "t" value 0.08 is not significant for df equal to 32. It indicates that the Mean Concept Development Test Gain Scores between boys and girls do not differ significantly from each other. So, the null hypothesis that "there is no significant difference in the Mean Concept Development Test Gain Scores of boys and girls" is not rejected. Further, the mean gain scores of boys and girls were 22.07 and 21.88 respectively. So, it was concluded that Advance Organiser Model is equally effective for the development of concepts of boys and girls in science.

DISCUSSION

The steps and techniques followed in Advance Organiser Model are equally effective for both boys and girls in the development of concepts in science.

4.10.0 DIFFERENCE IN THE ACHIEVEMENT BETWEEN BOYS AND GIRLS TAUGHT THROUGH ADVANCE ORGANISER MODEL.

The tenth objective is "to find out the difference in the achievement in boys and girls taught through Advance Organiser Model". The hypothesis corresponding to this objective is stated that "there is no significant difference in Mean Achievement Test Gain Scores of boys and girls taught through Advance Organiser Model". Keeping this hypothesis in mind the Mean Achievement Test Gain Scores were analysed with the help of "t" test between boys and girls. The results are given in table - 4.10.

Table - 4.10

"t" test in the Mean Achievement Test Gain Scores of boys and girls.

Group	Mean AT Gain Scores	SD	N	"t" value	Result
Boys	20.64	2.58	13	0.38	Not significant
Girls	20.96	2.01	21		

Not Significant

$df = n_1 + n_2 - 2 = 21 + 13 - 2 = 32$

From the table - 4.10, it was observed that the "t" value 0.38 is not significant for df equal to 32. It indicates that Mean Achievement Test Gain Scores between boys and girls don't differ significantly from each other. So, the null hypothesis "there is no significant difference in the Mean Achievement Test Gain Scores between boys and girls taught through Advance Organiser Model" is not rejected. Further, the mean gain scores of boys and girls were 20.64 and 20.96 respectively. So, it was concluded that the Achievement Test Gain Scores of boys and girls do not differ significantly from each other and the Advance Organiser Model is equally effective for the achievement of boys and girls in science.

DISCUSSION

The steps and techniques followed in Advance Organiser Model are equally effective for both boys and girls in achievement in science.

4.11.0 RELATIONSHIP BETWEEN INTELLIGENCE AND CONCEPT DEVELOPMENT

The eleventh objective is "to study the relationship between Intelligence and Concept Development in science of primary school students". The hypothesis corresponding to the objective stated that "there is no significant relationship between Intelligence and Concept Development Test Gain Scores in science". Keeping this hypothesis in mind the pretest scores of both Intelligence and Concept Development Test were analysed with the help of Product Moment Coefficient of Correlation Method. The formula of Product Moment Coefficient of Correlation is given below.

$$r = \frac{N\sum XY - \sum X . \sum Y}{\sqrt{\left\{N\sum X^2 - (\sum X)^2\right\}\left\{N\sum Y^2 - (\sum Y)^2\right\}}}$$

where X = Intelligence Scores
Y = Concept Development Test Scores
The result is shown in table - 4.11.

Table - 4.11

Correlation between Intelligence and Concept Development

$\Sigma X = 4164$ $\Sigma X^2 = 168554$ $\Sigma XY = 41358$ $N = 107$ $r = 0.96$ $\Sigma Y = 978$ $\Sigma Y^2 = 10742$

From table - 4.11, it was observed that the "r" value 0.96 is significant at 0.01 level because the calculated "r" value is more than the table value 0.19 at 0.01 level. It indicates that the relationship between Intelligence and Concept Development Test Scores are significant. So, the null hypothesis "there is no significant correlation between Intelligence and Concept Development Test Scores" is rejected. In other words, there exists relationship between Intelligence and Concept Development. It also indicates that the student with high intelligence develop high concepts in science.

4.12.0 RELATIONSHIP BETWEEN INTELLIGENCE AND ACHIEVEMENT

The twelfth objective of the present study is "to study the relationship between Intelligence and Achievement Test in science". The hypothesis corresponding to the objective stated that "there is no significant relationship between Intelligence and Achievement Test Scores in science". Keeping this hypothesis in mind, the pretest scores were analysed with the help of Product Moment Coefficient of Correlation method. The formula of Product Moment Coefficient Of Correlation is given below.

$$r = \frac{N\sum XY - \sum X . \sum Y}{\sqrt{\left\{N\sum X^2 - (\sum X)^2\right\}\left\{N\sum Y^2 - (\sum Y)^2\right\}}}$$

where X = Intelligence Scores
Y = Achievement Test Scores
The result is shown in the table – 4.12.

Table - 4.12

Correlation between Intelligence and Achievement

$\Sigma X = 4164$	$\Sigma X^2 = 168554$				
		$\Sigma XY = 31718$	$N = 107$	$r = 0.83$	
$\Sigma Y = 744$	$\Sigma Y^2 = 6888$				

From the table - 4.12, it was observed that the "r" value 0.83 is significant at 0.01 level because the calculated "r" value is more than the table value 0.19 at 0.01 level. It indicates that the relationship between Intelligence and Achievement Test Scores are significant. So, the null hypothesis "there is no significant relationship between Intelligence and Achievement Test Scores in science" is rejected. In other words, there exists relationship between Intelligence and Achievement. It also indicates that the students of high intelligence develop high achievement in science.

4.13.0 RELATIONSHIP BETWEEN CONCEPT DEVELOPMENT AND ACHIEVEMENT

The thirteenth objective of the present study is "to study the relationship between Concept Development Test and Achievement Test Scores in science of primary school students". The hypothesis corresponding to the objective stated that "there is no significant relationship between Concept Development Test Scores and Achievement Test Scores in science". Keeping this hypothesis in mind the pretest scores both Concept Development Test and Achievement Test were analysed with the help of Product Moment Coefficient Correlation method. The formula of Product Moment Coefficient of Correlation is given below.

$$r = \frac{N\sum XY - \sum X . \sum Y}{\sqrt{\left\{N\sum X^2 - (\sum X)^2\right\}\left\{N\sum Y^2 - (\sum Y)^2\right\}}}$$

where X = Concept Development Test Scores

Y = Achievement Test Scores

The result is shown in the table - 4.13

Table - 4.13

Correlation between Concept Development Test Scores and Achievement Test Scores.

$\Sigma X = 978 \qquad \Sigma X^2 = 10742$	
	$\Sigma XY = 8467 \quad N = 107 \quad r = 0.94$
$\Sigma Y = 744 \qquad \Sigma Y^2 = 6888$	

From the table - 4.13, it was observed that the "r" value 0.94 is significant at 0.01 level. Because the calculated "r" value is more than the table value 0.19 at 0.01 level. It indicates that that the relationship between Concept Development Test Scores and Achievement Test Scores are significant. So, the null hypothesis "there is no significant relationship between Concept Development Test Scores and Achievement Test Scores" is rejected. So, it was concluded that there is significant and positive correlation between Concept Development Test Scores and Achievement Test Scores. In other words, there exists relationship between Concept Development and Achievement. It also indicates that the students with developed concepts were high in achievement in science.

4.14.0 FINDINGS OF THE STUDY

The findings of the present study were stated below:

1. The treatment Concept Attainment Model is effective for the development of scientific concepts of primary students.
2. The treatment Concept Attainment Model is effective for the achievement of primary students in science.
3. The treatment Advance Organiser Model is effective for the development of scientific concepts of primary students.
4. The treatment Advance Organiser Model is effective for the achievement of primary students in science.

5. The treatment Concept Attainment Model is more effective than the treatment Advance Organiser Model for the development of scientific concepts of primary students.
6. Both the treatments, Concept Attainment Model and Advance Organiser Model are equally effective for the achievement of primary students in science.
7. The treatment Concept Attainment Model is equally effective for the concept development of boys and girls in science.
8. The treatment Advance Organiser Model is equally effective for the achievement of boys and girls in science.
9. The treatment Advance Organiser Model is equally effective for the concept development of boys and girls in science.
10. The treatment Advance Organiser Model is equally effective for the achievement of boys and girls in science.
11. The relationship between intelligence and concept development is positive and significant.
12. The relationship between intelligence and achievement is positive and significant.
13. The relationship between concept development and achievement is positive and significant.

4.15.0 SUGGESTIONS FOR THE FURTHER RESEARCH

1. The study was conducted on the sample of primary school students from Baripada municipality in the district of Mayurbhanj, Odisha. Similar study may be taken in other districts of Odisha as well as in other states.
2. The study was confined to teaching strategies of Concept Attainment Model and Advance Organiser Model from topics of science syllabus from class - IV. Similar study may be taken up by using different teaching strategies.
3. The present study was confined to primary level. Similar study may be conducted on other levels of learning like secondary and higher secondary levels etc.
4. The treatment Concept Attainment Model and Advance Organiser Model also be used for teaching other subject

like – Mathematics, English and Social studies etc. in different classes.

4.16.0 RECOMMENDATIONS

The study recommends as:

1. Concept Attainment Model and Advance Organiser Model help in the concept development and achievement of primary school students. Teachers may use these two strategies in teaching science at all levels.
2. Teachers should be oriented in the use of these two strategies i.e. Concepts Attainment Model and Advance Organiser Model for teaching science.

5.0.0 INTRODUCTION

In the previous chapter details regarding various aspects of this study have been given. In this chapter, the various aspects of the study have been presented in short.

5.1.0 STATEMENT OF THE PROBLEM

For the present study the problem is stated as follows:
"A study of effectiveness of Concept Attainment Model and Advance Organiser Model in the development of concept and achievement in science of primary school students".

5.2.0 OBJECTIVES OF THE STUDY

The following objectives have been undertaken:

1. To study the effectiveness of Concept Attainment Model in the concept development of primary students in science.
2. To study the effectiveness of Concept Attainment Model in the achievement of primary students in science.
3. To study the effectiveness of Advance Organiser Model in the concept development of primary students in science.
4. To study the effectiveness of Advance Organiser Model in the achievement of primary students in science.

5. To study the comparative effectiveness of Concept Attainment Model and Advance Organiser Model in the concept development of primary students in science.
6. To study the comparative effectiveness of Concept Attainment Model and Advance Organiser Model in the achievement of primary students in science.
7. To study the difference in the concept development between boys and girls taught through Concept Attainment Model in science.
8. To study the difference in the achievement between boys and girls taught through Concept Attainment Model in science.
9. To study the difference in the concept development between boys and girls taught through Advance Organiser Model in science.
10. To study the difference in the achievement between the boys and girls taught through Advance Organiser Model in science.
11. To study the relationship between intelligence and concept development.
12. To study the relationship between intelligence and achievement.
13. To study the relationship between concept development and achievement.

5.3.0 HYPOTHESIS OF THE STUDY

The following hypotheses have been undertaken:

1. There is no significant difference in the Mean Concept Development Test Gain Scores of Experimental Group - I (Ex_1) and Control Group - I (C_1).
2. There is no significant difference in the Mean Achievement Test Gain Scores of Experimental Group - I (Ex_1) and Control Group - I (C_1).
3. There is no significant difference in the Mean Concept Development Test Gain Scores of Experimental Group - II (Ex_2) and Control Group - II (C_2).

4. There is no significant difference in the Mean Achievement Test Gain Scores of Experimental Group - II (Ex$_2$) and Control Group - II (C$_2$).

5. There is no significant difference in the Mean Concept Development Test Gain Scores between Experimental Group - I (Ex$_1$) and Experimental Group - II (Ex$_2$).

6. There is no significant difference in the Mean Achievement Test Gain Scores of Experimental Group - I (Ex$_1$) and Experimental Group - II (Ex$_2$).

7. There is no significant difference in the Mean Concept Development Test Gain Scores between boys and girls taught through Concept Attainment Model.

8. There is no significant difference in the Mean Achievement Test Gain Scores between boys and girls taught through Concept Attainment Model.

9. There is no significant difference in the Mean Concept Development Test Gain Scores between boys and girls taught through Advance Organiser Model.

10. There is no significant difference in the Mean Achievement Test Gain Scores of boys and girls taught through Advance Organiser Model.

11. There is no significant correlation between Intelligence and Concept Development Test Scores.

12. There is no significant correlation between Intelligence and Achievement Test Scores.

13. There is no significant correlation between Concept Development Test and Achievement Test Scores.

5.4.0 SAMPLE OF THE STUDY

The sample of the study consisted of 107 students of class - IV belonging to four primary schools in the district of Mayurbhanj, Odisha. Among the four primary schools, two primary schools were taken as Experimental Groups and other two schools were taken as Control Groups for conducting the research. These four schools are co-educational and had sufficient facilities for the experimental study. In the present investigation two types of treatments were used. The first treatment was "Concept Attainment Model" (CAM) and the second one was "Advance Organiser Model" (AOM). From four schools, two schools were taken as Experimental Group - I and Experimental Group - II and other two schools were taken as Control Group - I and Control Group - II. The group-wise distribution of name of schools, total number of students, number of students in each teaching strategy and sex was given in below:

Table - 5.1
Group-wise distribution of total number of students, sex and number of students in each teaching strategy.

Sl. No	Name of the school	Total Number of students	Name of the school Number of students in each Treatment				Sex	
			CAM		AOM		M	F
			Ex_1	C_1	Ex_2	C_2		
1	Sanachatra Nodal U.P School	35	35				24	11
2	Badachatra Primary School	17		17			07	10
3	Budhikhamari Primary School	34			34		13	21
4	Bhugudakata Primary School	21				21	11	10
	Total	107	35	17	34	21	55	52

From the above table, it is clear that the sample of the study was 107 students of class IV belonging to four co-educational schools. From those schools, Sanachatra Nodal Primary School was selected to the first teaching strategy - Concept Attainment Model (CAM) and taken as Experimental Group - I (Ex_1), Budhikhamari Primary School was selected to the other teaching strategy - Advance Organiser Model (AOM) and taken as Experimental Group - II (Ex_2), and out of the rest schools, Badachatra Primary School was selected as Control

Group - I (C_1) and Bhugudakata Primary School was selected as Control Group - II (C_2), which were received the Traditional Method. The first Experimental Group was consist of 35 students, out of them24 were boys and 11 were girls. This Experimental Group was received the treatment of 'Concept Attainment Model'. The Control Group - I, which received the treatment of the 'Traditional Teaching Method' provided by the school teacher of the concerned subject, was consist of 17 students out of which 7 were boys and 10 were girls. Similarly, another Experimental Group was received the treatment of 'Advance Organiser Model', which was consist of 34 students. Out of which, 13 were boys and 21 were girls. The Control Group - II was also received the treatment of the 'Traditional Teaching Method' provided by the school teacher of the concerned subject, which was consist of 21 students out of which, 11 were boys and 10 were girls.

5.5.0   DESIGN OF THE STUDY

The present study was experimental in design. In this study, it was necessary to use "Two groups - pre-test - post-test - parallel group design". The main foucs of the present study was to make a study of the effectiveness of the Concept Attainment Model and Advance Organiser Model over Traditional Method, i.e. to make a comparative study of the effectiveness of two models of teaching over Traditional Method of teaching. For this purpose, there is the requirement of two Exprimental Groups and two Control Groups. The first teaching strategy was Concept Attainment Model and the second one was Advance Organiser Model. The Concept Attainment Model was developed by Bruner for better conceptualisation of the subject matter in the class room. And the second teaching model namely Advance Organiser Model was developed by David Ausubel which has great potential in teaching concepts, relationships, imparting and assimilating the information and ideas effectively and meaningfully. For this purpose four schools were selected for the study.

For conducting the experiment 30 lesson plans were prepared separately for each teaching strategy from unit II to IX of class IV science syllabus. The lesson plans were prepared according to the phases or steps of the each teaching strategy. These lesson plans were taught in both the experimental groups through the procedure of CAM and AOM teaching strategies. It means treatments were followed in the Experimental Groups and the Traditional Method was followed by the two Control Groups. To measure Intelligence of the students, an Intelligence test version by Dr. Rama Tiwari was translated into mother tongue Odia language. To measure the development of concepts and achievement of the students, a Concept Development Test in Science (CDTS) and an Achievement Test in Science (ATS) were developed and standardised by the investigator with the help of the guide. All these tests were also printed in the press. For administration of tests and teaching lessons, a time-table was prepared for each school after consulting with the concerned Headmasters.

After adequate preparation and planning, on the first day the Intelligence Test was administered on the students of each school. On the second day, the Concept Development Test in Science was administered in each school and on the third day, Achievement Test in Science also administered in each school. All the above three tests were administered as pre-tests in three successive days in each school. After the pre-tests were conducted in four schools, the experimental groups were taught by the investigator according to the treatments and the control groups were taught by the concerned school science teacher according to the Traditional Method. Each type of teaching strategy was imparted for thirty classes of 45 minutes for 10 weeks. Hence, both the experimental treatments were completed within ten weeks.

After the experimental treatments were imparted, the following post-tests were administered to all the experimental and control groups.

1) Concept Development Test in Science (CDTS)
2) Achievement Test in Science (ATS)

These tests were administered on two successive days. The schematic diagram of the design is presented in the below table.

Table - 5.2
Schematic Diagram of the Design

Activity	Time	Ex$_1$ (CAM)	C$_1$ (Control Group I)	Ex$_2$ (AOM)	C$_2$ (Control Group II)
Pre-tests were administered	3 days	1) IT 2) CDTS 3) ATS	1) IT 2) CDTS 3) ATS	1) IT 2) CDTS 3) ATS	1) IT 2) CDTS 3) ATS
Teaching of 30 lessons on science subject of class - IV from unit-II to IX	10 weeks	CAM was used	Traditional Method was used	AOM was used	Traditional Method was used
Post-tests were administered	2 days	CAM was used	1) CDTS 2) ATS	1) CDTS 2) ATS	1) CDTS 2) ATS

5.6.0 TOOLS USED

In order to draw any valid conclusion from an experimental research, tools used for the measurement of variables should be reliable and valid. This requirement is usually met by employing standardised tests. Since, no research has been done in the area selected for the research, the researcher constructed her own test for the purpose. The present study required the following tools and measures.

1) Intelligence Test (IT)
2) Concept Development Test in Science (CDTS)
3) Achievement Test in Science (ATS)

5.7.0 INTELLIGENCE TEST

Intelligence Test or General Mental Ability Test (GMAT) was constructed and standardised by Dr. Rama Tiwari, Agra University, Agra; Published by Agra Psychological Research Cell (APRC). It is a test of verbal intelligence which consists of 70 questions. The included sub-tests are:

(i) Classification or spotting the stranger.
(ii) Number series.
(iii) Analogy
(iv) Problem solving
(v) Choosing
(vi) Reasoning or logical solution
(vii)Numerical ability

To evaluate the student's intelligence level "General Mental Ability Test" (GMAT) already constructed and standardised for the pupils of age range from 13 to 18 years was administered on the sample which consisted of both 'Experimental Groups' and 'Control Groups' numbering 107 students including both boys and girls.

The test was a speed test comprising seventy (70) test items which were all multiple choice type questions. Each question carries equal weightage of one (1) mark. So the full marks was 70 and the allotted time was 20 minutes. As the standardised question paper on 'General Mental Ability Test' was originally constructed in English, it was translated in to Odia by the investigator to suit age, ability and comprehension of the students whose mother tongue is Odia.

5.8.0 CONCEPT DEVELOPMENT TEST

The Concept Development Test was constructed by the Investigator. This test covered the units selected from the Science text book of class IV prescribed by the Orissa Board of Primary and Mass-education. The content areas also classified according to the different objectives to evaluate the various abilities of the students of Class - IV. There were 50 items in the test. Each item is followed by two examples, which are either positive or negative. In the answer sheet for each example there are two spaces for giving answer. The first space is given for the positive example and the second space is given for negative example. The students are directed to read the statement and to put tick mark () for positive example, if it is right and put tick mark () for negative example, if it is wrong at appropriate place. Each correct answer to the positive and negative examples carries one (1) mark. The maximum mark is 50 and the time limit of the test is 40 minutes.

5.9.0 ACHIEVEMENT TEST

The Achievement Test constructed by the investigator. The test item also covered the following science units selected from the text book of Science prescribed by Orissa Board of Primary and mass-education. The content areas also classified according to different objectives to evaluate various abilities of the student of class - IV.

The researcher selected the test-items from the selected areas, keeping in mind the predetermine objectives. There were 40 items in the test. The test included fill in the blanks, multiple choice, completion type, find out the odd one and matching types of items. Instructions regarding giving answers to question were written in clear and unambiguous terms or words. Marks was individually allotted to the question according to the difficult level of the question. Both marks and difficulty level were determined according to the judgement, experience and insight of the researcher. The maximum mark is 40. The time limit for the test is 40 minutes.

5.10.0 PROCEDURE OF DATA COLLECTION

After construction and standardisation of Concept Development Test and Achievement Test, the investigator made proper planning for administration of the Intelligence Test along with the Concept Development Test and Achievement Test on the sample of 107 students selected from four co-educational Primary schools of Baripada to carry out her study. The Headmasters and concerned teachers were contacted and with their consent a time-schedule was prepared for administration of these 3 tests as pre-tests. As stated before, all students of four schools of class - IV were included in the sample. The following tests were administered before the treatment as pre-tests.

1. Intelligence Test (Standardised)
2. Concept Development Test on Science
   (Constructed by the investigator)
3. Achievement Test on Science
   (Constructed by the investigator)

After the treatment was over, the same Concept Development Test and the Achievement Test were re-administered on the same students as post-tests.

1. Concept Development Test on Science
2. Achievement Test on Science

After the completion of these tests, the answer scripts were examined by the investigator. The scores in these tests were the only data used in the study.

5.11.0 STATISTICAL ANALYSIS

After scoring the test, Mean (M), Standard Deviation (SD) of the scores were obtained. Significance of difference between mean scores of different groups as well as of the same groups in the pre-tests and post-tests were determined and the co-efficient of correlation was calculated between scores of different variables to find the nature of relation if any between them.

5.12.0 FINDINGS OF THE STUDY

The findings of the present study were stated below:

1. The treatment Concept Attainment Model is effective for the development of scientific concepts of primary students.
2. The treatment Concept Attainment Model is effective for the achievement of primary students in science.
3. The treatment Advance Organiser Model is effective for the development of scientific concepts of primary students.
4. The treatment Advance Organiser Model is effective for the achievement of primary students in science.
5. The treatment Concept Attainment Model is more effective than the treatment Advance Organiser Model for the development of scientific concepts of primary students.
6. Both the treatments, Concept Attainment Model and Advance Organiser Model are equally effective for the achievement of primary students in science.
7. The treatment Concept Attainment Model is equally effective for the concept development of boys and girls in science.
8. The treatment Advance Organiser Model is equally effective for the achievement of boys and girls in science.
9. The treatment Advance Organiser Model is equally effective for the concept development of boys and girls in science.
10. The treatment Advance Organiser Model is equally effective for the achievement of boys and girls in science.
11. The relationship between intelligence and concept development is positive and significant.
12. The relationship between intelligence and achievement is positive and significant.
13. The relationship between concept development and achievement is positive and significant.

5.13.0 SUGGESTIONS FOR THE FURTHER RESEARCH

1. The study was conducted on the sample of primary school students from Baripada municipality in the district of Mayurbhanj, Odisha. Similar study may be taken in other districts of Odisha as well as in other states.

2. The study was confined to teaching strategies of Concept Attainment Model and Advance Organiser Model from topics of science syllabus from class - IV. Similar study may be taken up by using different teaching strategies.
3. The present study was confined to primary level. Similar study may be conducted on other levels of learning like secondary and higher secondary levels etc.
4. The treatment Concept Attainment Model and Advance Organiser Model also be used for teaching other subject like – Mathematics, English and Social studies etc. in different classes.

5.14.0 RECOMMENDATIONS

The study recommends as:

1. Concept Attainment Model and Advance Organiser Model help in the concept development and achievement of primary school students. Teachers may use these two strategies in teaching science at all levels.
2. Teachers should be oriented in the use of these two strategies i.e. Concepts Attainment Model and Advance Organiser Model for teaching science.

5.15.0 IMPLICATION OF THE STUDY

Science is one of the core subjects in school education. The need to make science teaching interesting and effective is, therefore, felt all around. In this context, educational psychologists like Bruner and Ausubel have developed two different theories of teaching based on which models of teaching evolved, namely - Concept Attainment Model and Advance Organiser Model. These strategies are considered to be effective in teaching scientific concepts. This investigation has been an attempt to test the effectiveness of these strategies - Concept Attainment Model and Advance Organiser Model in teaching science in common Indian school conditions.

From the present experimental study, it has been found that both Concept Attainment Model and Advance Organiser Model are found effective over Traditional Method of teaching in terms of concept development and achievement in science of primary students, which indicate that these models of teaching should be applied in Indian classroom teaching. The aim of these models of teaching should not only to acquaint the learner with the knowledge of science subject but also conceptual awareness has equal importance in the present day of scientific world.

ABBREVIATION

AOM	-	Advance Organiser Model
ATS	-	Achievement Test in Science
BSIM	-	Biological Science Inquiry Model
C_1	-	Control Group - I
C_2	-	Control Group - II
CAM	-	Concept Attainment Model
CAS	-	Concept Attainment Score
CDTS	-	Concept Development Test in Science
DIT	-	Defining Issue Test
Ex_1	-	Experimental Group - I
Ex_2	-	Experimental Group - II
GMAT	-	General Mental Ability Test
IT	-	Intelligence Test
ITM	-	Inquiry Training Model
JIM	-	Jurisprudential Inquiry Model
LPLM	-	Linear Programmed Learning Material
M	-	Mean
MCDT	-	Moral Concept Development Test
MPI	-	Maudsley Personality Inventory
MRCAMOT	-	Modified Reception Concept Attainment Model of Teaching
OCM	-	Operant Conditioning Model
PASTE	-	Process Appraisal Scale of Teacher Effectiveness
PLM	-	Programmed Learnig Material
PVQ	-	Personal Value Questionaire

Dr. Sasmita Mohanty

SD	-	Standard Deviation
TAG	-	Teaching Analysis Guide
TM	-	Traditional Method
TT	-	Traditional Teaching

BIBLIOGRAPHY

Alexander, L. (1977). 'A Study of the Effects of Advance and Post-Organizer of Learning and Retention of Oral Instruction, Dissertation Abstract International, Vol.38, No5, 1977.

Al-Sulman (1987). 'A Study of Earth Concept Attainment of Urban and Rural Saudi Arabian Social Studies Students'. Vol. 48, No.6, 1987. 1430 A.

Aman, Stanley Gane, Ed. D. (1981). The Influence of an Advance Organizer on Transfer in a Programmed Instruction Situation for Ninth Grade Industrial Arts Students. Anburn University, Dissertation Abstract University, Vol. 42, No. 8. 1982, p. 3473.

Antimadas (1986). "Effectiveness of Training Strategy in Concept Attainment Model and Personality of Pre-service Teacher Training". Trend of Research and Abstracts of Research Studies at M.Ed., M.Phil., Ph.D. and Project Levels at Department of Education: Trend Report and Abstract (1985-1986). Department of Education, Devi Ahilya Vishwavidyalya, Indore, M.P., 1987, p.42.

Ausubel, D.P. (1960). 'The Use of Advance Organizers in the Learning and Retention of Meaningful Verbal Material', Review of Educational Research, Vol. 45, No. 4, 1975.

Ausubel, D.P. and Fitzgerald, D. (1961). 'The Role of Discriminability in Meaningful Parallel Learning and Retention. Review of Educational Research. Vol. 45, No.4, 1975.

Ausubel, David P. and Fitzgerald, Donald (1962). 'Organizer, General, Background and Antecedent Learning Variables in Sequential Verbal Learning'. Journal of Educational Psychology, 1962, Vol. 53, No. 6, pp. 243-249.

Ausubel, D.P. and Youssef, D. (1963). 'The Role of Discriminability in Meaningful Parallel Learning the Retention'. Review of Educational Research, Vol. 45, No. 4, 1975.

Balley, Harald J. Ph.D. (1974). "Toward a Theory of Sequencing" – Study 4-1 : An Examination of the Effects of a Particular Cannical Teaching Procedure on Concept Attainment and Generalization in Mathematics. The Pennsylvania State University, Dissertation Abstract International, Vol. 36, No. 1, 1975, p. 98.

Barbara, A.N. (1973). "Effects of Analytic-Global and Reflexivity-Impulsivity Cognitive Styles on the Acquisition Geometry Concepts Presented Through Emphasis or No Emphasis and Discovery Lessons". University of Wisconsin Dissertation Abstract International, Vol. 33, No. 9, 1973, 4949-A.

Barnes, B.R. and Clawson, E.V. (1975). 'Do Advance Organizers Facilitate Learning? Recommendations for Further Research Based on An Analysis of thirty-two Studies'. Review of Educational Research, 1975, 45, pp. 637-659.

Barrow, Lloyed Harley, Ph.D. (1973). 'A Study of the Effect of an Advance Organizer in an Activity-Centred Science Program". The University of Iowa, Vol. 35, No. 1, 1974.

Bartel and Heckman, C.F. (1980). 'The Effect of Advance Organizers Versus High Human Interaction on P.S.I. Mastery Learning Programme in Nursing'. Dissertation Abstract International, Vol. 41, No. 4, 1980.

Benton, E.R. (1977). 'The Relationship between the Number of Attributes and the Number of Moves in Conjunctive Concept Teaching Strategy'. Texas University, 1976, Dissertation Abstract International, Vol. 37, No. 8, 1977, 4927-A.

Bernt, F.M. (1986). 'The Effects of Perceptual Differentiation and Conceptual Organization Upon Children's Hypothesis Testing Behaviour'. Dissertation Abstract International, Vol.47, No.3, 1986.

Bihari, S.K. (1986). 'Effectiveness of Training Strategy in Learning Concept Attainment Model at B.Ed. Level.' Trend Report and Abstract (1985-86). Department of Education, Devi Ahilya Vishwavidyalaya, Indore, M.P., 1987, P.53.

Brune, Patrica Anne. Ed.D. (1982). Effects of Advance Organizers on Listening Comprehension among Learning Disabled and Non-Learning Disabled Adolescents. The University of Alabama, Dissertation Abstract International, Vol.44, No.2, 1983, P.456.

Buddhisagar, Meena, Ph.D. (1986). "Development and Comparison of Instructional Material Developed by Using Advance Organizer Model and Operant Conditioning Model for Teaching Educational Psychology to B.Ed. Students". Trend Report and Abstract (1985-86), Department of Education, Devi Ahilya Vishwavidyalaya, Indore, M.P., 1987, P.62.

Carol, Keller, Ed.D. (1968). The Effects of Cognitive Operational Levels, Instructional Feedback, and Retention over Time on Concept Attainment. The University of Flordia, Dissertation Abstract International, Vol.30 No.1, 1969, P.210.

Charles, R.L. (1978). 'The Effects of Instancing and Prompting Moves on the Learning Two Mathematical Concepts, Indiana University, 1977, Dissertation Abstract International, Vol.38, No.9, 1978, 5309 A.

Chitrive, U.G. (1983). 'Evaluating Differential Effectiveness of Ausubel and Brunner Strategies for Acquisition of Concepts in Mathematics'. In Ausubel vs. Brunner Model for Teaching Mathematics. Himalaya Publishing House, Bombay, 1988.

Clibrun, J.W. (1985). 'An Ausubelian Approach to Instruction : the Use of Concept maps as Advance Organizers in a junior College Anatomy and Physiology Course', Dissertation Abstract International, Vol.47, No.3, 1986.

Corbelt, J.V. (1985). 'The Effects of two types of Preinstructional Strategies on two levels of Cognitive Learning from a written study unit for undergraduate Nursing Students'. Dissertation Abstract International, Vol.47, No.2, 1986.

Dalton, Michaelleon, Ph.D. (1986). "The thought Process of Teachers when Practicing Two Models of Teaching". University of Oregon, Dissertation Abstract International, Vol.47, No.9, 1987, P.3400.

Darrow, Donald Richard, Ph.D. (1980). "The Relative Effectiveness of an Advance Organizer on the Meaningful Verbal Learning and Retention of Junior High School Students in Industrial Arts", The Ohio State University, Dissertation Abstract International, Vol. 42, No. 7, P.4315.

Das, Bishnucharan, M.Phil. (1986). "Effectiveness of CAM in Terms of Teaching Competency of Pre-Service Student- teachers". Trend Report and Abstract (1985-86). Department of Education, Devi Ahilya Vishwavidyalaya, Indore, M.P., 1987, P.44.

Dena, Carol Marie, Ph.D. (1980). "The Effects of Using a Graphic Advance Organizer Before, During and After Reading on the Comprehension of Written Text, a Study Conducted with Sixth Grade Students". The University of Wisconsin Madison. Dissertation Abstract International, Vol. 42, No. 7, P.4344.

Derr, K.T. (1978). 'Advance Organizers : A Comparison of the Effectiveness and Efficiency of Behavioural Objectives and Sample Test, Dissertation Abstract International, Vol. 39, No. 3, 1978.

Doyle, W.H. (1981). 'Using an Advance Organizer to another Subsuming Function Concept to Facilitate Learning, Transfer and Retention in Remedial College Mathematics'. Dissertation Abstract International, Vol. 42, No. 5, 1981.

Fulton, Anne Ware, Ph.D. (1981). An Investigation of the Effectiveness of Selected Teaching Strategies Integrating the Teaching of Science Concepts and the Improvement of Reading Language Skills, University of Southern Mississippi, Dissertation Abstract International, Vol. 42, No. 8, P. 3533.

Gangrade, (Ms) Archana (1987). 'Comparison of Combination of Concept Attainment Model and Lecture Method with Traditional Method for Teaching Science to Classes VII and VIII Students'. Department of Education, Devi Ahilya Vishwavidyalaya, Indore, M.P., 1987.

Giles, T.W. (1981). 'A Comparison of Effectiveness of Advance Organizers and Clustering Singly and in Combination upon Learning in the Planetarium'. Dissertation Abstract International, Vol. 42, No. 1, 1981.

Gonzales, R.F. (1982). 'A Comparison of the Effects of Advance Organizers on Retention of Technical Content', Dissertation Abstract International, Vol. 43, No. 7, 1983.

Groteluescher, A and Sjogren, D.G. (1968). 'Effects of Differentially Structured Introductory Materials and Learning Task on Learning Transfer'. Review of Educational Research, Vol.45, No.4, 1975.

Haghighi F. (1981). 'The Effects of Underlined Cues, Advance Organizers, and Post-Organizers on Meaningful Prose Learning'. Dissertation Abstract International, Vol. 42, No. 3, 1981.

Jachobson, L.I. (1969). 'Relationship of Intelligence and Mediating Process to Concept Learning'. Journal Educational Psychology, 1969.

Johnson, A.N. (1985). 'Influence of Verbal and Non-verbal Mediation on the Identification of Stylistic Similarities in Paintings'. Dissertation Abstract International, Vol. 46, No. 2, 1985, 332-A.

Jooly, E.D. (1978). 'A Study of the Use of Laboratory Approach in the Teaching of Selected Concepts of Perimeter, Area and Volume to Seventh Grade Students'. Auburn University, 1977, Dissertation Abstract International, Vol. 38, No. 11, 1978, 6568-A.

Jones, Edwaed Everett, Ed.D. (1974). The Comparative Effects Level of Specific Advance Organizers on the Achievement of Students of Differing Ability Levels. Oklahoma State University, Dissertation Abstract International, Vol. 35, No. 10, 1975, P.6529.

Josephson, D.A. (1978). 'Interaction of an Advance Organizer and Perceptual Style in the Learning and Retention of Mathematics. Dissertation Abstract International, Vol. 39, No. 4, 1978.

Kennedy, Keith A. (1974). 'The Effectiveness of a Comparative Advance Organizer in the Learning and Retention of Metric System Concepts'. The University of Lowa Dissertation Abstract International, Vol. 35, No. 12, Part I, 1975, 7786.

Klausmeir and Davis (1970). Cognitive Style of Concept Identification as a Function of Complexity and Teaching Procedure, I.Edn. 1970.

Kornriech L.B. (1969). 'Solving Concept Identification Problems', Journal of Educational Psychology, No.60, 1969, 384-388

Lalli, E.D. (1980). 'The Use of Advance Organizers as a Method to Reduce State Anxiety and Improve Performance on Teacher Made Test'. Dissertation Abstract International, Vol. 41, No. 5, 1980.

Lasky, Beth Anne (1986). 'Advance Organizers as an Instructional Strategy for Bilingual Learning Disabled Students'. The University of Arizona, Dissertation Abstract International, Vol. 47, No. 11, 1987, 4056-A.

Lemke, Elmer Allen, Ph.D. (1965). "The Relationship of selected Abilities to Some Laboratory Concept Attainment and Information Processing Task". The University of Wisconsin, Dissertation Abstract International, Vol. 28, No. 3, 1967, P.967.

Lemke, W.R. (1980). 'A Comparison of the Effectiveness of a Programmed Instruction Techniques Using Advance Organizers and Study Questions as Ancillary Learning Activities for Brass Technique Classes at the College Level'. Dissertation Abstract International, Vol. 40, No. 12, 1980.

Lenz, B.K. (1983). 'The Effect of Advance Organizer on the Learning and Retention of Learning Disabled Adolescents within the context of a Cooperative Planning Model'. Dissertation Abstract International, Vol. 44, No. 4, 1983.

Mahajan, Sharmila Roy, Ph.D. (1983). "The Differential Effects of Ausubelian Advance Organizers on the Learning of Students Characterized as Formal Operational and Concrete Operational in the Piagetian Paradigm, the University of Texas at Austin. Dissertation Abstract International, Vol. 4, 1983, P.1065.

Maher, Phillip Ray, Ph.D. (1975). "The Effects of Advance Organizers on the Interpretative Level of Reading Comprehension of Selected Fourth and Sixth Grade Students". The University of Akron. Dissertation Abstract International, Vol. 36, No. 5, 1975, P.2616.

Martin, D.A. (1980). 'The Effect of an Advance Organizer on Student Learning of Economic Concepts at the University Level'. Dissertation Abstract International, Vol. 41, No. 7, 1981.

Mascolo, Richard Peter (1967). Key Conceptual Schemes and Inquiry Training : Some Effect Upon New Learning. New York University, Dissertation Abstract International, Vol. 25, No. 4, 1967, P.1345.

Meena, V.G. (1979). 'The Effects of Written and Graphic Comparative Advance Organizers Upon Learning and Retention from Audio-Visual Presentation'. Dissertation Abstract International, Vol. 40, No. 7, 1980.

Mills, Bruce Frank Ph.D. (1973). The Function of Motivation in Concept Attainment : A Teaching Model. Indiana State University, Vol.34, No.9, 1974, P.5804.

Miller R. (1980). 'The Use of Concrete and Abstract Concept by Children and Adult'. Dissertation Abstract International, Vol. 41, No. 5, 1980.

Miller, Ronald, E. (1984). 'A Study of the Effects of Visual Organizers on Learning nad Retention. University of Northen Colorado, Dissertation Abstract International, Vol. 45, No. 6, 1984, 1704.

Mills, H.R. (1973) Teaching and Training : A Handbook for Instructors. N.Y., Macmillan, (1973).

Morgan, Barbara Small, Ph.D. (1985). The Effects of Two Types of Prelaboratory Exercises when used as Advance Organizers on Student Achievement and Abilities in an Introductory Biology Laboratory Course". Georgia State University, Dissertation Abstract International, Vol. 46, No. 12, Part 1, 1986, P.3673.

Noel, Kent, Ph.D. (1983). The Effects of Advance Organizers on Transfer of Rule Learning". The Florida State University, Dissertation Abstract International, Vol. 44, No. 12, 1983, P. 471.

Oeballos, Elva Guajardo, Ph.D. (1986). "Effects of Concept Teaching Methods on Cognitive Thinking Ability". The University of Texas at Austin, Dissertation Abstract International, Vol. 47, No. 9, 1987, P. 3292.

Oppong, Jacob Emmanuel, Ed.D. (1978). A Study of Advance Organizer and its Effects on Achievement of Ninth Grade Social Studies Students". University of Georgia, Dissertation Abstract International, Vol. 39, No. 12, 1979, P. 7275.

Panda, Bibhutibhusan (1986). "A Comparative Study of the Effect of Advance Organizer and Set Induction on Learning". Trend of Research and Abstract of Research Studies at M.Ed., M.Phil., Ph.D. and Project Levels at Department of Education, Trend Report and Abstracts (1985-86). Department of Education, Devi Ahilya Vishwavidyalaya, Indore, M.P., 1987, P.43.

Pandey, A., Ph.D. Edn. (1981). "Teaching Style and Concept Attainment in Science". Third Survey of Research in Education (1978-1983). 1987, P.769.

Pani, Pushpanjali (1983). "A Study of Comparison Between Reception and Selection Strategies of Concept Attainment". Trend of Research and Abstract of Research Studies at M.Ed., M.Phil., Ph.D. and Abstracts (1985-1986), Devi Ahilya Vishwavidyalaya, Indore, M.P., 1987, P. 39.

Passi, B.K. Singh, L.C., D.N. Sansanwal (1985). "Effectiveness of Strategy of Training in Models of Teaching in Terms of Understanding, Reactions and Willingness of Teacher Educators". (Sponsored by NCERT, New Delhi) Phase I in Trend Report and Abstract (1985-86). Department of Education, Devi Ahilya Vishwavidyalaya, Indore, M.P., 1987, P. 69.

Passi, B.K. Singh, L.C., D.N. Sansanwal (1986). 'Implementing Training Strategies and Studying Effectiveness of Different Variations in Components of Training Strategy for CAM/ITM in Terms of Understanding, Competence, Reactions and Willingness of Student-Teachers'. (Sponsored by NCERT, New Delhi) Phase II in Trend Report and Abstract (1985-86). Department of Education, Devi Ahilya Vishwavidyalaya, Indore, M.P., 1987, P. 70.

Passi, B.K. Singh, L.C., and Sansanwal, D.N. (1986). 'Adopting Training Strategy and Studying Effectiveness of Different Variations in Components of Training Strategy for Cam/ITM in Terms of Understanding Competence, Reactions and Pupil Liking'. (Sponsored by NCERT, New Delhi) Phase III in Trend Report and Abstract (1985-86). Department of Education, Devi Ahilya Vishwavidyalaya, Indore, M.P., 1987, P. 72.

Peters, Charles Warren, Ph.D. (1973). A Comparison Between the Frayer Model of Concept Attainment and the Text Book Approach to Concept Attainment. The University of Wisconsin. Dissertation Abstract International, Vol. 34, No. 9, 1974, P. 5599.

Pathania, R.S. (1980). 'An Experimental Study of the Effectiveness of Advance Organizers in relation to Creativity, Scholastic Achievement'. Unpublished M.Ed. Dissertation, Department of Education, Indore University, 1980.

Peley, Z.R. and Moor, R.F. (1980). 'Effects of Advance Organizer with Oral and Written Permutation on Recall and Inference of E.M.R. Adolescents'. American Journal of Mental Deficiency, Vol.86, No. 6, 1982.

Rajoriya, (Miss) Renuka, M.Phil. (1987). 'Comparison of Advance Organizer Model with Traditional Method for Teaching Science to Class VIII Students with Different Residential Background". Department of Education, Devi Ahilya Vishwavidyalaya, Indore, M.P., 1987.

Rechards, J.P. and Mc Carnik, C.B. (1977). 'Whole Versus Part Presentation of Advance Organizers in Text'. Journal of Educational Research, Vol. 70, No. 3, 1977.

Rodgers, C.A. (1981). 'Using a Comparative Advance Organizer: The Effect of Indentified Relationship on Expository for Success'. Dissertation Abstract International, Vol. 41, No. 12, 1981.

Rodman, S.M. (1982). 'The Differential Effect of Advance Organizers and Behavioural Objectives on Achievement in aBasic Statistics Course'. West Virginia University, Dissertation Abstract International, Vol. 43, No. 3, 1982, P. 736.

Rottavina, Paul John, Ph.D. (1977). The Relationship among Concept Attainment Skills, Academic Achievement and Classroom Adjustment in Socially Maladjusted Youth, The University of Connecticut, Dissertation Abstract International, Vol. 39, No. 11, 1978, P. 6701.

Satapathy, Biranchinarayan (1987). 'Relative Effectiveness of Wholist Partist and Partst-first Demonstration Approaches in Training Student-Teachers in Advance Organizer Model'. Trend Report and Abstract (1985-86). Department of Education, Devi Ahilya Vishwavidyalaya, Indore, M.P., 1987.

Scandura, J.M. and Well, H.N. (1967). 'Advance Organizers in Learning Abstract Mathematics'. Review of Educational Research, Vol. 45, No. 4, 1975.

Schulz, R.W. (1966). 'The Role of Cognitive Organizers in the Facilitation of Concept Learning in Elementary School Science'. Review of Educational Research, Vol. 45, No. 4, 1975.

Schutz, Samuel Roy, Ph.D. (1969). Rule and Attribute Learning in the Use and Identification of Concepts with Young Disadvantaged Children. University of California, Los Angeles. Dissertation Abstract International, Vol. 30, No. 11, 1970, P. 4838.

Schwartz, P.J. (1979). 'The Effect of Prior Knowledge Subsumers and Advance Organizers on the Bearing of Unfamililar Science-related Material at the College Level'. Dissertation Abstract International, Vol. 40, No. 7, 1980.

Saggie, J.L. (1969). 'Level of Learning Involved Disjunctive Concepts'. A.J.P., 9, 1969.

Senapati, Sanjukta (1986). 'The Effect of B.Ed. Students' Personality Characteristics on Achievement Taught Through Programmed Learning Material, Advance Organizer Material, and Traditional Method". Trend Report and Abstract (1985-86). Department of Education, Devi Ahilya Vishwavidyalaya, Indore, M.P., 1987. P. 53.

Sharma, Vibha (1986). "Effectiveness of Concept Attainment Model in Terms of Pupil Achievement and their Reactions". (Sponsored by NCERT, Bhopal) Trend Report and Abstract (1985-86). Department of Education, Devi Ahilya Vishwavidyalaya, Indore, M.P., 1987, P. 78.

Smith, C.D. (1976). 'The Effects of Organizers and Abstract Reasoning Levels on Learning and Retention of Post-Secondary Mathematics Student'. Dissertation Abstract International, Vol. 37, No. 6, 1976.

Stankiewiez, J.J. (1984). 'The Effects of Advance Organizer on the Ability of Randomly Selected Groups of Seventh and Eighth Grade Science Students to Recall and Apply Facts after a Visit to a Science Museum'. Temple University, Dissertation Abstract International, Vol. 45, No. 1, 1984, 14-A.

Stiff, L.V. (1978). 'The Effect of Pure C and E Strategies, Number of Moves, and Relevant Knowledge on Learning a Contrived Algebric Concept". North Carolina State University at Raleigh, 1978, Dissertation Abstract International, Vol. 39, No. 5, 1978, 2803-A.

Sushma (Km) (1987). 'Effectiveness of Concept Attainment Model and Biological Science Inquiry Model for Teaching Biological Science to VIII Class Students'. Department of Education, Banaras Hindu University, Varanasi, 1987.

Thredgill, J.A.M. (1977). 'The Relationship of Analytic-Global Cognitive Style and two Methods of Instruction in Mathematics Concept Attainment. University of Oregon, 1976, Dissertation Abstract International, Vol. 37, No. 9, 1977, 5664-A.

Wager, Walter William, Ed.D. (1972). "The Relative Efficiency and Effectiveness of Three Objectives Rules of Sequence Applied to a Concept Attainment Task". Indiana University, Dissertation Abstract International, Vol. 33, No. 11, 1973, P. 6244.

Watkins, Rosemary Cannon, Ph.D. (1982). "The Effect of Ausubel's Advance Organizer Model on the Acquisition of Fundamental Music Concepts and Skills by Non-Music Majors". The University of Texas Austin, Dissertation Abstract International, Vol. 43, No. 7, 1983, P. 2272.

Weisberg, Joseph Simpson, Ed.D. (1969). "The Use of Visual Advance Organizers for Learning Earth Science Concepts, Columbia University, Dissertation Abstract International, Vol. 30, No. 9, 1970, P. 3867.

Wilson, J.C. (1980). 'Differential Effects of a Comparative Advance Organizers on Performance, Attitude and Practice in Learning a Dance Skill'. Dissertation Abstract International, Vol. 41, No. 1, 1980.

Worthen, B.R. (1968). 'Discovery and Expository Task Presentation in Elementary Mathematics'. Journal of Educational Psychology, Monograph Supplement, Vol.59, 1968, 1-13.